"The Harris brothers have helped shatter the stereotype of the narcissistic, self-involved teenager. They, and the sea of students who share their passion for God and for changing the world, are leading the body of Christ by their example, not by their words. That's why the words they've written in *Start Here* have such power to change a teenager's life—they're merely describing what's possible, from firsthand experience...and it's highly motivating!"

—DOUG FIELDS, youth pastor at Saddleback Church
and founder of Simply Youth Ministry

"Alex and Brett Harris are not impressed with themselves; they're impressed with God. And they're not afraid to get their hands dirtied up in the service of God's blue-collar rescue operation. That's a recipe for freedom—for 'doing hard things.' *Start Here* is a strategic field manual for young people who feel a burning desire to spend their *only* priceless asset—their own lives—to buy their way into God's rebel uprising on earth. Alex and Brett call it The Rebelution. The Bible calls it the advance of the kingdom of God. I call it radically inspiring."

—RICK LAWRENCE, executive editor of *Group Magazine*
and author of *Jesus-Centered Youth Ministry*

"Where *Do Hard Things* was an inspiring call to action, *Start Here* is the hands-on guidebook for a new way of living and leading. Alex and Brett know how to motivate young adults to live intentionally, think big, and aim high—and they do it with style. I highly recommend *Start Here*. It's a book that will change how you think, what you dream about, and what you choose to do next."

—BRAD LOMENICK, vice president of Giant Impact
and executive director at Catalyst

Praise for
Do Hard Things
by Alex and Brett Harris

START HERE

START HERE

DOING HARD THINGS

RIGHT WHERE YOU ARE

ALEX&BRETT HARRIS

with Elisa Stanford

MULTNOMAH
BOOKS

START HERE
PUBLISHED BY MULTNOMAH BOOKS
12265 Oracle Boulevard, Suite 200
Colorado Springs, Colorado 80921

All Scripture quotations, unless otherwise indicated, are taken from The Holy Bible, English Standard Version, copyright © 2001 by Crossway Bibles, a division of Good News Publishers. Used by permission. All rights reserved. Scripture quotations marked (NIV) are taken from the Holy Bible, New International Version®. NIV®. Copyright © 1973, 1978, 1984 by International Bible Society. Used by permission of Zondervan Publishing House. All rights reserved.

Italics in Scripture quotations reflect the authors' added emphasis.

All the stories in Start Here come from real young people around the world. Their words have been edited for style and length but not for content. Used by permission.

ISBN 978-1-60142-270-5
ISBN 978-1-60142-271-2 (electronic)

Published in the United States by WaterBrook Multnomah, an imprint of the Crown Publishing Group, a division of Random House Inc., New York.

MULTNOMAH and its mountain colophon are registered trademarks of Random House Inc.

Library of Congress Cataloging-in-Publication Data
Harris, Alex, 1988–
    Start here : doing hard things right where you are / Alex and Brett Harris ; with Elisa Stanford. — 1st ed.
        p. cm.
    Companion book to: Do hard things.
    Includes bibliographical references and index.
    ISBN 978-1-60142-270-5 — ISBN 978-1-60142-271-2 (electronic)
    1. Self-actualization (Psychology)—Religious aspects—Christianity. 2. Self-actualization (Psychology) in adolescence. 3. Expectation (Psychology)—Religious aspects—Christianity. 4. Adolescent psychology. I. Harris, Brett, 1988– II. Stanford, Elisa. III. Title.
    BV4598.2.H365 2010
    248.8'3—dc22

                                                    2009047280

Printed in the United States of America
2010 — First Edition

10 9 8 7 6 5 4 3 2 1

SPECIAL SALES
Most WaterBrook Multnomah books are available at special quantity discounts when purchased in bulk by corporations, organizations, and special-interest groups. Custom imprinting or excerpting can also be done to fit special needs. For information, please e-mail SpecialMarkets@WaterBrookMultnomah.com or call 1-800-603-7051.

—

To our grandmothers, Lily Sato and Frances Harris,
thank you for all your love and prayers.

To Randy Alcorn,
a faithful mentor and a living hero.

CONTENTS

YOU ARE HERE

Opening the door to your own rebelution

Simple ideas and unbelievable dreams. First steps and great miracles. Ordinary teenagers and a God who still uses young people to accomplish His big plans.

That's what our first book, *Do Hard Things,* is all about. *Do Hard Things* shows how young people can take hold of a more exciting option for their teen years than what society suggests. We wrote the book to counter the Myth of Adolescence, which says the teen years are a time to goof off and have fun before "real life" starts. We invited our peers to choose to do hard things for the glory of God and, in the process, turn the world's idea of what teens are capable of upside down.

We were nineteen when we wrote *Do Hard Things,* twin brothers who wanted to follow God's call and challenge our generation. We're twenty-one now and sophomores in college. We still dream big dreams, still want to follow God completely, and still believe just as strongly that God wants to use our generation to change the world. (And, as you might have guessed, we're still twin brothers.)

Whether or not you've read *Do Hard Things* (we'd recommend it—but, of course, we're a little biased), this companion book continues the *Do Hard Things* message and piles on stories, practical suggestions, and detailed how-tos. You can use it either on your own or in a group setting, depending on your situation.

In other words, *Do Hard Things* marked the beginning of a movement. *Start Here* is your personal field guide to jumping in and getting involved.

The Rebelution Movement

The concept of doing hard things actually started as a blog we created when we were sixteen. We called it The Rebelution—a combination of *rebellion* and *revolution* to create a whole new word with a whole new meaning. We defined *rebelution* as "a teenage rebellion against low expectations." (By the way, the blog still exists. Check it out at TheRebelution.com.)

Since *Do Hard Things* came out, the Rebelution movement has exploded. In the past year, rebelutionary teens have raised tens of thousands of dollars to bring the gospel to and dig wells in Africa, won prestigious film festivals, fought human trafficking in the United States and around the world, and made it on the cover of *ESPN The Magazine*. Around the world, young people are moving out of their comfort zones—whether that means standing for Christ in a hostile classroom, raising money to build a dormitory for orphans in China, or mending relationships with parents or younger siblings.

Maybe you're part of the Rebelution already, or maybe you

just want to find out more. Maybe you're asking one of the questions we get most frequently from readers: "Where do I start?"

This book is about taking the next step. It includes ideas from us and dozens of other young people on topics like:

- how to stand up for what you believe
- strategies for overcoming stage fright, fund-raising fright, and phone-calling fright (hint: it gets easier as you go!)
- ways to get going when you feel stuck and keep going when you feel discouraged
- how to understand God's will and glorify Him through your efforts
- God-honoring ways to think, feel, and act *after* you've completed a big project

In short, this is a handbook full of practical steps and real-life stories to encourage and equip you on your journey of doing hard things. We want you to feel as if you're at one of our conferences, or in a small group of people talking about doing hard things—which you may be!

All the questions in the pages that follow come from people just like you, collected on our website and through personal conversations. We'll do our best to answer them with stories and insights from our own lives. We're traveling alongside you in this adventure—and we want to share with you what God has been teaching us these past few years.

But just like *Do Hard Things*, this book isn't about us. It's about the incredible, seemingly impossible things God is doing in our generation. That's why in *Start Here* you'll find dozens of true stories from rebelutionaries who are making a difference in their homes, at their schools, and around the world. We love sharing other young people's stories because they challenge us as well—and remind us that we're not alone. We also love the way real-life stories provide a glimpse of the diverse ways God wants to use each of us to do hard things for Him.

Toward the end of the book, we'll be sharing the stories of two rebelutionaries in particular: Ana Zimmerman and John Moore. As you'll see, Ana and John took on very different hard things, each with the purpose of glorifying God and helping others.

At the age of fifteen, Ana raised more than six thousand dollars and organized an event called Love the Least in her hometown. The event introduced her community to the work of Abort73, an organization that exists to show the injustice of abortion.

With a group of fellow teens, John Moore wrote, produced, and directed his own feature film at the age of nineteen—and went on to win the $101,000 grand prize at the San Antonio Independent Christian Film Festival.

John and Ana faced many of the same hurdles and questions you're encountering. Their stories provide an in-depth look at the beginning, middle, and end of the "do hard things" process. We think you'll be encouraged and inspired.

Pursuing Faithfulness, Not Success

As thousands of young people around the world are discovering, doing hard things is the most satisfying, thrilling way to live some of the best years of our lives.

So where do you start? As you'll find in the pages that follow, the answer is: right where you are. Being a rebelutionary means committing to doing even ordinary things extraordinarily well.

As each of us is faithful in that, God will be faithful to prepare us for whatever calling He has for us.

For some of us, that calling will be big in the world's eyes, and for some of us it will be small. Whether it is big or small, God will be glorified—and the world will be changed by a generation that gives up seeking worldly success to pursue a life of faithfulness.

That's when the ordinary becomes extraordinary. And that's what this book is about.

Ready to start?

GETTING STARTED

What that first step looks like

If you're feeling lost in trying to figure out where to start, you might be asking practical questions about how to create a plan, get others involved, and make your project work. Those are good questions, and we'll be tackling all of them (and more) in the next chapter. But most of the time, those *aren't* the right questions to be asking—at least not at first.

The best question to ask right at the beginning is "*Why* am I doing hard things?" When we remember that we're doing hard things to glorify God and become more of who He created us to be, it puts the "How do I start?" question in a different light.

As you think and pray about what God wants *you* to be doing, keep in mind that you don't have to fight God in order to do hard things. He *wants* you to do hard things! The Bible says that He has prepared good works for you and has prepared you for those good works (see Ephesians 2:10). God is far more concerned about His glory, your good, and the good of those around you than you are. That means you don't have to engineer something—you can trust Him, be faithful, and be ready for *His* timing.

So here are some thoughts on responding to what God is already eager to do in your life.

I'm ready to get started—on *something*! What should I do now?

When we think or talk about doing hard things, it's easy to think only about the big stuff. If we assume that being a rebelutionary means fighting slavery, digging wells in Africa, running a political campaign, or writing a book, then it *is* hard to know where to begin!

But if our goal is to glorify God—to point other people to Him and show more of what *He* can do—then our first priority is to be faithful with what He's *already given us to do,* not embark on a big new adventure. *What* we're doing doesn't necessarily change right away, but *how* and *why* we're doing it will change dramatically.

Let us introduce you to the first of many real-life stories we'll be using in this book. As you'll see in Elisabeth's story, the place we start doing hard things is right where God has us already— such as sitting in a car on a snowy night.

I was ready to go out and conquer hard projects. Big responsibilities. Things far outside my comfort zone. I prayed for God to work through me in big ways. He answered me, but not quite in the ways I expected.

For instance, one night on the way home in a blizzard, my dad and I stopped for a few minutes to pick up some necessities at the store. I waited in the car and surveyed the nearly empty parking lot until my eye caught a lone car with a person scraping off snow. As I looked closer,

I saw that it was an elderly lady trying to scrape off her car while leaning on a cane. She wasn't making much progress because the snow was falling faster than she could wipe it off. I felt instinctively that I had to help her. I ran out with my scraper, and soon a few other people joined me in clearing off her car.

Nothing outwardly significant happened then, but this was the first time I had strongly heard God's voice and responded to it. As I tuned in, I began to recognize His voice at other times. I sensed that I should go talk to the girl who was crying in the bathroom at school—it turns out she was pregnant and needed help. Or that I should offer tips to someone who was trying out for the sports team—it turns out she needed advice on deeper areas of her life that she normally wouldn't have opened up about.

What I have found is that in order to do hard things and conquer big challenges, we need to be willing to listen to that little voice the Holy Spirit uses. The more you listen, the clearer it becomes. And in order to do the great things, you must first be a servant.

—Elisabeth, age 17
Raymond, Maine

Even though Elisabeth had dreams about the hard things *she* wanted to be doing, she was tuned in to God's voice when He spoke. God answered her in ways she didn't expect, but she was ready to hear Him. And with one simple act of obedience, Elisabeth became aware of many other opportunities for doing hard things.

When your heart and mind are alert, you can see opportunities to do *hard things* in *everyday things*. It might start with a renewed commitment to excellence in your schoolwork or a decision to help more around the house. School and chores are things you probably do already, but now, as a rebelutionary, you are doing them with a new attitude. Your primary goal isn't to do something extraordinary but to do all things, even the ordinary things, extraordinarily well.

We want rebelutionaries to dream big, but we've also observed that God often passes over the person with grand, me-focused plans in favor of the one who has a heart to love others, to trust Him, and to do the small things for their own sake.

Doing hard things doesn't mean being preoccupied with something bigger, different, and more exciting all the time. It means being ready and willing to obey, no matter how big, small, or hard it might be. Elisabeth's openness to God's leading made her available to several unexpected opportunities to show the love of Christ. Faithfulness in small hard things is always the fuel for bigger hard things.

If we say we want to do hard things for God, but we're not satisfied with pursuing excellence where He has placed us (at home, at school, and at work), it's likely that we're really more interested in getting glory for ourselves than in getting glory for Him.

So where do you start? Right where you are—with a new attitude, a new heart, and a mind open to how the everyday hard things available to you right now will lead you to the next step.

How can I tell the difference between good hard things in general and good hard things I should be doing?

Every rebelutionary has asked this question at one time or another. We know *we* have, whether it was when we were trying to decide if God was calling us into filmmaking the summer before we started the Rebelution (He wasn't) or when we were trying to decide whether to write this book the summer between our freshman and sophomore years at college (we did).

Sometimes the struggle is due to the fact that there are so many options and so many needs. We know God doesn't call us to do *everything*, but we don't know how to identify the things we *are* supposed to do.

Charity's story offers some great ideas and questions for discerning what hard thing to tackle next:

> Ever since I was about eight years old, I have loved to crochet. I often made things as gifts for newborn babies. I had been pondering for a couple years how I could serve others through crocheting but never came up with a concrete plan.
>
> Once I heard about the idea of doing hard things, I thought I should quit trying to come up with a perfect idea and just do something simple. So I decided to collect handmade hats for orphans overseas. After talking to my parents about my idea, I came up with a plan to collect two hundred hats by Christmastime. That gave me three months to carry it out.
>
> I live in a small town of eight hundred people, and at that time I could count on one hand how many people

I knew who could knit, crochet, or sew. This meant that I would either have to make way more hats than I possibly could or I would have to find people who I didn't know to make hats. There was a little doubt in my mind as to whether this could happen, but I put it in God's hands and let Him decide the outcome.

I realized that I needed to get in contact with someone who could distribute the hats for me. For years, I've packed shoe boxes for Operation Christmas Child, which is part of Samaritan's Purse, an organization that sends gifts and necessities to children overseas. I have always dreamed of helping them distribute those boxes someday. I couldn't think of a better organization to distribute the hats.

After getting things figured out with Samaritan's Purse, I began to collect the hats. First, I posted my idea on The Rebelution.com. To my amazement and delight, quite a few girls promised to make hats and send them to me for the project. They were all so encouraging and energetic that it made the project a lot of fun. Many of them invited their friends to help out. One was even able to get her school to make hats! Another girl told her mother and grandmother, and together the three generations made over forty beautiful hats.

As I talked to other people where I live, many wanted me to teach them to crochet in order to make a hat. Not only did these people learn how to crochet and give me a couple hats, but they also continued crocheting and are now still making things and giving them away as gifts. I never dreamed anything like that would happen, but it did.

By December, I had over three hundred and fifty hats to send to Samaritan's Purse. People from Australia, Japan, and the United States donated to this project. I can't believe it when I think of all the people who donated. I didn't even know the names of many of them. Isn't it great how God can use the simplest idea and make it a success?

    —Charity, age 18

    Glennallen, Alaska

Take a look at some of the questions Charity asked as she set out to do hard things.

What Do I Like to Do?

Serving God does *not* mean being miserable. Yes, doing hard things is challenging, but as Charity discovered, it often involves doing something we are gifted at and something we enjoy. God may be calling you to something totally outside your current area of interest or expertise, but it's more likely He's calling you to *take the next step* with something you're already doing.

If people comment on how welcoming you are to others, could God be calling you to reach out to new students at your school? Maybe you're good at making an argument but hate public speaking—could God be calling you to use your gift of debate to stand up for a good cause? Or maybe, like Charity, you have a talent or hobby that could be used to serve others in a greater way.

In other words, you don't start doing hard things just *where* you are but also with *who* you are. The gifts, interests, and talents God has given you all provide clues to what hard things He is calling you to do.

Who Can Help Me Think This Through?

Proverbs 20:29 says that the glory of youth is "their strength" and that the glory of the old is their "gray hair"—or accumulated wisdom (NIV). As young people, we have a lot of energy, but we don't always know what to do with it. Sometimes we have trouble choosing among all the options. If we're not careful, we can even use our strength in ways that are destructive to ourselves and others by moving forward without considering the implications of our actions. That's why God gives us parents, older siblings, teachers, pastors, and mentors to help us tell the difference between a good hard thing, and a good hard thing *we* should be doing.

Charity found encouragement as well as practical advice when she turned to her parents with her idea. They helped her settle on a solid goal for how many hats to collect and provided a sounding board for her ideas.

As you work to understand God's calling, seek out the advice of others who are living godly lives—and who can share the wisdom of their own life experiences.

Would This Conflict with the God-Given Obligations I Have?

God is good, and because He is good, He doesn't give us conflicting obligations. There will always be enough time to do everything He has given us to do—and no time to waste.

As young people, we're in the season of preparation. Our main focus during this season is to prepare for mature, effective adulthood: work, marriage, family, service to others, leadership, and ministry. This doesn't mean that we can't work, lead, or minister to others as students, but those things are not the main focus. Our preparation is.

Understanding this concept changes our question from the fuzzy "Is this hard thing something *I'm* supposed to do?" to the more helpful "Does this help me to prepare for adulthood or distract me from my preparation?" If it is a distraction, you shouldn't feel bad about passing on it. Sometimes doing hard things means saying no.

As an eight-year-old, Charity may not have been ready to organize a hat drive for orphans overseas, but those years learning to crochet prepared her for a hard thing God called her to do as a teenager. Faithfulness in one season prepares us to step into the next season with strength. Who knows what God is preparing for her (and for you) next?

In chapter 3, we'll be looking at a few more guidelines for when to say yes and when to say no to a specific hard thing. For now, remember that being faithful in the season of preparation means saying yes to some hard things and no to others. More specifically, it means saying yes to preparation and no to distraction.

But don't overanalyze. If God gives you an opportunity to do a hard thing, your parents or godly mentors are supportive, and it doesn't conflict with your other God-given obligations, trust God and go for it! Just as He did for Charity, He will provide what—and who—you need to fulfill this new responsibility.

What if I just want to join other people in what *they* are doing?

In America we're taught to admire the rebel and the loner. While going against the flow of a lost culture is good, allowing the go-it-alone mentality to pervade our thinking can be dangerous.

Because whether we're leading or assisting in a project, it's not about us.

I've loved computers forever. Looking back, I don't know what made me contact Leslie and Lauren Reavely about designing a website for their organization, H2O, but I did. That's obviously where God was working "behind the scenes."

H2O—which stands for Hope 2 Others—distributes lunch bags to homeless people and panhandlers across the country.[1] I didn't have a ton of experience in web design (I was thirteen), but I was willing to help.

I honestly thought Leslie and Lauren would reply with a no since I'm some guy on the other side of the country who they don't know. Also, I'm not really talkative or a very good communicator. But somehow God was able to use me to reach out and help these two girls who were doing incredible things for God.

We launched the new Hope 2 Others (H20Bags.com) site on New Year's Day last year. It's been amazing to see the response. We had over five hundred unique visitors within the first couple months, and the response continues to grow.

I must admit, it hasn't always been easy. During the six months it took to get the site going, God enabled me to overcome the fear I had of communicating with people I didn't know. He helped me get through all the uninteresting parts of designing the site that I would've preferred to skip. He also taught me perseverance.

Then last April, my family and some good Christian friends started a church plant. My dad pastors it, and last

November I designed the website. My mom and I were up until six the morning we launched it. While only about thirty people attend our church each week, God has richly blessed us.

Recently, other people have asked me to work on their websites as well. It's quite different having someone come to me versus the other way around. But God is doing amazing things, and I'm thankful that He has allowed me to be part of them.

—Matthew, age 15

Charlottesville, Virginia

God didn't make us to be independent but *inter*dependent. Think about a nation, a business, an army, a sports team, or a family. A quick look around shows clearly that we were created to depend on others and have others depend on us. Matthew offered his gifts to others—and the founders of H2O were humble and wise enough to receive them.

As young people, we're called to do hard things as part of the family team in particular. We honor and obey our parents by joining them in the work they're doing—whether it's putting on an event at church or cleaning up the yard.

What is your family doing right now that you could be an active and willing part of? It doesn't have to be helping with a church plant like Matthew did. Teaming up with your family might mean doing something as simple as having a good attitude about setting the dinner table or taking care of your siblings so your parents can take a break.

Yet even more important than our role in our family or on a

team is the fact that we are part of the church—the body of Christ. The apostle Paul wrote, "God has so composed the body...that there may be no division in the body, but that the members may have the same care for one another. If one member suffers, all suffer together; if one member is honored, all rejoice together" (1 Corinthians 12:24–26).

We're *all* part of someone else's project: God's. As brothers and sisters in Christ, we are called to be united, striving side by side for the gospel. Rather than caring about who gets the credit, we're commanded to "outdo one another in showing honor" (Romans 12:10). God's plan is for us to work together in community.

It can often be harder to work with others than it is to work on our own. We have to share the credit, deal with people who are sinful and crabby, and let others see our own faults and short-comings. But joining with others to do God's work is the way His biggest plans get accomplished. It's also one of the best ways for us to grow in Christlike character and bring glory to Him. And that's why we do hard things.[2]

So as you try to follow God's calling, remember that you don't have to be doing your own thing to be doing something hard for God. God might be calling you, as He did Matthew, to join someone else who needs help with a hard thing.

Do small hard things really count?

To answer this question, take out the word *small*. Do hard things really count? Of course! Remember, *small doesn't mean easy*. We should still be stepping outside our comfort zones, going above and beyond expectations, and doing what is right, even if our actions don't seem all that impressive to most people. Why? Because big or small, the hard things God calls us to do are about Him, not us.

That's why, to fully answer the question, we have to ask a bigger one: what *ultimately* counts? If the answer is "being famous" or "what people think about me," then small hard things don't matter much. But when we read God's Word, we find that small things have great significance, not just to prepare us for bigger things, but also for their own sake. And sometimes small hard things are the hardest things of all.

In Colossians 3:23, Paul writes, "Whatever you do, work at it with all your heart, as working for the Lord, not for men" (NIV). In 1 Corinthians 10:31, he writes, "Whether you eat or drink or *whatever you do,* do it all for the glory of God" (NIV). What Paul is saying is that everything—even something as simple as befriending someone in gym class—can be done for God's glory. And that means *nothing* we do for God is insignificant.

This year I started attending a new public high school. It was in one of my PE classes during the first month of school that I began noticing the "outsiders." As part of the class, we had to warm up by running five or six laps around the school track. For most of the kids in the class, including me, this was no problem. But not everyone was in the greatest shape after a long summer.

After finishing my laps, I was standing around and saw a girl who was behind everyone else. She was struggling to keep up. At first I didn't give her a second thought, but as I saw how much she was hurting, the Lord put her on my heart. I sensed that God was saying, *Hannah, I want you to go run with her!*

I felt really, really weird. I immediately argued back, *What, Jesus? Are You serious? I've never even spoken to that girl! I don't even know her name!* But I knew I had to obey Him, even though everyone else in the class might think I was dumb.

So, saying a silent prayer, I jogged out to the girl. She was crying and struggling to breathe, but her face radiated with surprise and thankfulness as I came up beside her. Even though I didn't know her, the love of the Lord brought us together, and we finished those laps strong.

—Hannah, age 17
Chesapeake, Virginia

We doubt anyone in Hannah's class patted her on the back, and her story certainly didn't make the newspaper. Was it still worth it? It depends on how you answer the question we asked earlier: what ultimately counts?

The *Westminster Shorter Catechism* (an early Q and A about Christian beliefs) says, "What is the chief end of man? To glorify God and enjoy Him forever." That means that simple acts of obedience, like Hannah's, matter a lot. It also means that it is possible to dazzle people with the hard things we do and still waste our lives if we're doing those things only to impress others and bring glory to ourselves.

Small hard things might have "small" results in this life, but as Paul encourages, "Let us not grow weary of doing good, for in due season we will reap, if we do not give up" (Galatians 6:9).

God will bring a harvest—whether in this life or the next—if we persevere in the everyday things He has given us to do at school and at home.

Do you feel God calling you to do something big for Him? Don't despise the day of small beginnings. Not only are big hard things usually made up of a lot of small hard things put together (so you're getting good practice!), but also God has a way of opening new opportunities when we least expect it.

Big hard things often start with one small step. Just ask Jaime Coleman.

A few years ago, Jaime's church partnered with a missions organization that uses humanitarian projects to share the gospel in rural Kenyan communities. Her church adopted the town of Karogoto, and Jaime soon discovered a pressing need in the town for something that most of us take for granted: shoes.

Jaime figured that her family wasn't the only one with shoes in the closet they didn't need. She set a goal to collect 150 pairs of shoes. Her plan was to kick off the drive with a Barefoot Mile at her high-school's track. People would come, donate shoes, and walk four laps around the track barefoot. Some adults questioned whether anyone would show up—but it didn't take God long to prove them wrong.

"There were definitely low expectations," Jaime tells us. "It was discouraging, but I knew God could make it happen. On a rainy Saturday, fifty people showed up at the track—with 1,164 pairs of shoes! By the time the drive was over, God had brought in over 4,200 pairs of shoes for the people of Karogoto."[3]

Why do we share Jaime's story in response to a question about "small" hard things? Because Jaime didn't set out to collect 4,200 pairs of shoes. Her desire was to participate in the work of her local church. Her goal was small: 150 pairs of shoes. And even now, when we talk to her, she refuses to take credit for what God has done.

Stories like Jaime's remind us that God wants (and will use) faith, humility, and availability—not glory seeking, pride, or a preoccupation with our own ideas. If Jaime had thought, *A few dozen pairs of shoes isn't going to make enough of a difference,* she would have missed a chance to see God do *incredible* things with a simple idea. If Hannah had second-guessed God's prompting to do a "small" hard thing in gym class that day, she would have missed an opportunity to show His love to someone else.

Nothing we do for God is insignificant. When we have this as our mind-set, then we won't get proud if God allows us to do something big and we won't get discouraged if we feel stuck in the small things. Remember, neither fame nor obscurity is the goal. The goal is obedience to God, effectiveness in whatever He gives us to do, and a heart that glorifies Him.

Whether we are called to live life on a big stage or behind the scenes, we cannot forget the words of Jesus in Matthew 23, who modeled this mind-set for us: "The greatest among you shall be your servant. Whoever exalts himself will be humbled, and whoever humbles himself will be exalted" (verses 11–12).

I know God wants me to do something with this idea, but I'm not ready for it now. What can I do to get ready for doing this hard thing later?

What do you mean when you say, "I'm not ready"? If you mean, "I don't feel adequate," you might just be making an excuse. No one is adequate to do the kinds of things God calls us to do. In fact, God tends not to use people who feel adequate because they are usually full of pride.

Are you really meaning, "I'm afraid," or, "My motivations aren't pure enough"? The day will never come when we stop feeling afraid and our motivations are perfectly pure. True courage is not the absence of fear; it is refusing to allow our fear to control our actions. And while keeping our motives in check is a constant battle, good motives now are better than perfect motives when it's too late. (As one rebelutionary told us, "When I am scared or unsure about doing something hard, I think about the person I want to be when I am older and how doing this hard thing will help me become more like that person.")

On the other hand, if you're saying, "God has put something on my heart but wants me to be patient about beginning it," this might be a season of preparation rather than completion. Preparing *now* to do a particular hard thing *later* is not only helpful on a practical level, but it also keeps you prayerful and alert to see when the right time comes.

What parts of your project suggest that you need to wait? Do you need more time, money, or experience than you have now? What *is* available to you now?

For example, maybe you feel that God is calling you to make a film that honors Him, but the specific project you have in mind is way beyond your current resources or abilities. You know you want to do it, but you're not sure you can do the project justice until you've gained further experience. Ask yourself what practical things you could be doing now to prepare for the day when you can complete that hard thing: What smaller projects might you tackle in order to gain the skills you'll need later? Who could you seek as a mentor in this field? How should you be praying about the future?

Ian's story captures another aspect of what we're saying here:

Last year, when my dad was in the hospital, I realized that there was no hope for him on Earth. I turned to the only person who could help him: Jesus.

I made my way from my dad's bedside to the hospital chapel to pray. The door was locked. That was how I felt. Locked out from God and locked out from hope.

Thursday, May 13, Dad died. The funeral came and went, and my grades started to slip. I was usually pretty good in school, but now I was doing the bare minimum, just enough to pass each class.

Every Friday night, I went to a youth club in my church, but I never took much interest in it. Then one night we went to a Christian festival. I was blown away by the amazing worship, the amazing sermon, and the amazing thought that was planted in my head—that God really does love me, the guy who doubted Him, the guy who put out little effort at school, the guy who never loved Him.

At the end of the night, there was an appeal for those who wanted to accept Jesus as their Savior. I grappled internally. My heart told me that I loved Jesus and wanted to take Him in. My mind told me that it was too big a commitment to make. That night my heart won.

I went away that evening with hopes of seeing my dad again. He was a Christian, and I realized that a Christian

friendship doesn't end with death—death is just a brief
pause in an eternity-long friendship.

When I told my minister that I had become a Christian, he gave me a copy of *Do Hard Things*. After reading
the book, I had a vision of changing the future, but I realized that I would have to change myself first.

So instead of scraping by, I am now releasing my full
potential. I am working hard to get good grades in every
class I take. I learned how to play the guitar, and I play in
my church's praise group several times a week. Every day
I encounter obstacles, peer pressure, and temptation. But
every day of my new life is a blessing. I hope, by the example I set, that others will come to know Jesus and live a life
for Him.

—Ian, age 16
Belfast, Northern Ireland

"I had a vision of changing the future," Ian says, "but I realized that I would have to change myself first." Doing hard things
involves a paradox: we dream big about changing the world, and
we believe that God will help us do it. And we have to start with
ourselves, right where we are. If that means putting "bigger"
plans on hold for a time, we can still look for ways that God can
prepare us for those plans right now.

WHEN YOU HAVE A GREAT IDEA

Practical help for making it work

Once you start doing the hard things God has put right in front of you, He might give you an idea for a brand-new challenge or a bigger vision for what you are already doing. At this stage, you probably have a lot of questions—and that's a great place to start.

When we decided to start doing Rebelution conferences in 2006, we had a ton of questions. We'd never organized an event before, spoken in public for more than ten minutes straight, or coordinated a team of volunteers from hundreds of miles away.

But as we asked questions (and asked for help!), things started coming together. Today we've hosted sixteen regional conferences attended by over thirty-five thousand teens, parents, and youth workers. Our comfort zones have expanded—and we've learned a lot.

This chapter brings together many of the very practical lessons we and other rebelutionaries have learned along the way.

What kind of planning do I need to do before I launch this thing?

Sixteen-year-old Joshua Guthrie had read that nine hundred million people around the world face death because of a lack of clean water. He'd heard that water-related disease kills more than 3.5 million people each year, the great majority of them children.

He knew he wanted to do something.

He started by talking with a family friend who led Baptist Global Response, an international relief and development organization working with just the kind of ministry goals that Joshua had. Joshua got advice on what it would take to drill a well in Sudan and tips on how to raise money.

"I thought that paying for a well would be a cool thing to do, but a teen really can't save up eight or ten thousand dollars for a well," Joshua says. "I knew I would have to raise it with the help of others."[1]

Joshua decided he would ask fellow teens to give up one drink so they could give one dollar to help build one well. His goal was to raise eight thousand dollars by Christmas. With his parents' support, he reserved a domain name, registered his new organization—Dollar for a Drink—as a nonprofit, and got a website up.

The fund drive took off—not through large donations, but through churches and individuals across the country giving one-, five-, and ten-dollar bills. By Christmas, Dollar for a Drink had raised more than ten thousand dollars. The final check to Baptist Global Response totaled over eleven thousand dollars. Now six thousand people in Sudan—who previously had to walk four hours to get clean water—draw water from the well this money bought.

"I learned you actually have to take the first step forward," Joshua says. "Starting something like this was kind of intimidating. But Dad and I sat down and made a list of five things we needed to do. They were real simple things, and then we just kind of got going with it."

Joshua's next hard thing is to raise twenty-four thousand dollars to drill three wells in Sudan. "You've got to trust God that it's possible to do something like this," he says. "So often people think, *Well, that person is exceptionally gifted,* or, *That person really had the right resources. I couldn't do that.* I'm just a completely ordinary guy, but I serve an extraordinary God. It's possible for God to use you, if you'll let Him do His work."

Joshua Guthrie could have chosen many ways to help people in Africa—he settled on a fairly *big* goal! But with the help of others, he asked the questions needed to accomplish his goal. These are good questions for all of us to consider, especially when the hard thing we are called to do involves the money, time, and efforts of a lot of people.

What Are My Limits?

An important part of embarking on a project is knowing how to scale it to what you can realistically do. Recognizing your limitations does not mean questioning what God can accomplish through you or restricting yourself to doing what comes easily. It means practicing wisdom.

For example, it's better to set a goal to feed a few hundred people at your local homeless shelter *and do it* than to set a goal to solve world hunger and not accomplish anything. After all, as you are faithful to do what you can creatively and effectively, God might turn your outreach to the homeless in your community into something that reaches the poor and hungry around the country—and even around the world. When we focus on doing what we can do with excellence, it can open the door for God to do the impossible.

A good exercise in planning a hard thing is to first ask yourself the question, *What would I do if I had unlimited time and unlimited resources?* That question helps you identify the big target—your vision as large as it can be.

Then ask yourself, *What could I do toward reaching that goal within the limitations I face?*

Finally, in light of the answers to the first two questions, ask yourself, *What should I do?*

The first question is a visionary question about what you *would* do. The second is a practical question about what you *could* do. And the third is a moral question about what you *should* do. All three questions are important.

Joshua's huge vision might be to provide clean water for the entire continent of Africa. Within his limitations, he was able to raise money to dig one well that provides drinking water to several African villages. Now he is increasing his goal slightly and hoping to raise money for three wells next year. By not allowing what he would *like* to do to get in the way of what he *can* do, Joshua is leaving the door open for God to do even greater things through him.

What Do I Bring to the Table? What Can Others Contribute?

Before you begin, ask yourself what experience or skills you have that relate to the things you want to do. What parts of your project will you need the most help with, and what will come most easily?

Asking these questions requires you to be honest about your strengths and weaknesses and to be thoughtful about which people can fill in the gaps where your knowledge or ability falls short. Joshua had the passion to help provide drinking water to people in Africa, but he learned from others how to do it and why it was needed.

Remember not to overlook the "home field advantage." Do any of your family members or extended family members have particular skills, resources, or connections that could help you? How might your siblings be good team members? How could your parents or grandparents mentor you in your challenge?[2]

You can also learn from those who are working in a different field but have expertise in some part of your project—filing for nonprofit status, for instance, or making T-shirts, or getting group rates on transportation. Gleaning information from others frees you to devote more time to moving your big idea forward.

What Are Others Already Doing? What Can I Learn from Them?

As we suggested in chapter 2, if you like what others are doing and think joining them would be more effective than starting from scratch, become a part of their efforts! You might be just the encouragement (and boost of energy) they need.

But as you explore what is currently being done, be sure to ask yourself, *What is missing?* Take advantage of your novice eyes. You will be able to look at situations in ways that people who have been involved for years might not be able to. Be teachable and quick to listen to those who are more experienced, but don't be afraid to ask questions like, "Why do we do it this way and not that way? Can it be handled differently?" If the answer is, "Well, that's just the way we've always done it," then you may have stumbled across an opportunity to be a real game changer. You might also find that a crucial niche is being unaddressed by existing groups and organizations.

Whether you join with someone else, as Joshua did, or start out on your own with your new knowledge, understanding what already exists will help you refine your original plan if you need to.

Who Knows More than I Do About This?

We can learn a lesson from the Old Testament account of the queen of Sheba—the foreign ruler who sought out King Solomon in order to benefit from his wisdom (see 1 Kings 10:1–13). We should seek out those individuals who are at the top of the field we want to enter. These people usually write books or articles or speak at conferences related to the topic. They may be relatively unknown outside their field, but within their field, they are among the most highly respected voices.

Once you have identified these individuals, take advantage of the material they have already made available. Read their books; listen to their talks; visit their websites. Then make a solid attempt to contact them or even meet in person—maybe at an event where they are speaking.

Whenever you meet someone you admire, one of the first things you want to be able to say is, "I've read your book(s)." These men and women like to talk to people who have been good stewards of what they have already said or done. Then you will have the opportunity to share your vision and ask them the best question in the world: "What would you do if you were me?"

What Can I Read About This Topic?

Our dad always told us, "If you read the three best books on any given topic and you really think about and digest the contents, then you will be more qualified in that area than 99 percent of the world." Now, we don't think anyone ever did a scientific study to prove our dad right or wrong, but we're pretty sure the principle is true regardless of the exact percentage.

Once you find the Solomon in your field, ask him or her to recommend the three best books on your topic—and then read them. You won't learn everything you need to know, but you will be in a much better position to see your hard thing through.

Also, keep in mind that the best resources might not be books. You might need to subscribe to scholarly journals or read an industry magazine. Whatever the biggest mouthpiece of the movement is, find it, read it, and put its words into practice.

What Is My Goal?

Right from the beginning, envision what your project will look like one year from now. Then walk backward from that vision to the present, answering questions along the way until you get to where you are.

For instance, "One year from now, a new well in Africa will provide clean drinking water to thousands of people. Which means I need to figure out who needs that well the most and how much it will cost. Which means I need to figure out who is building wells right now. Which means…"

Depending on your project, you might envision what it will look like in three, five, ten, and fifty years as well, always working backward to the steps you need to take today.

It's not that things won't change. Part of going from plan to action is dealing with the reality of actually getting things done. You might find that what you think will be the hardest part is actually the easiest and what you think will be a breeze turns out to be the most discouraging. But taking the time to think ahead, prepare for challenges, and set goals will help you follow through on what God has called you to do. As Dwight D. Eisenhower once said, "In preparing for battle, I have always found that plans are useless, but planning is indispensable."

How do I Move from Planning to Doing?

After all this talk about planning, recognizing your limits, and seeking counsel, we still want to encourage you not to get so caught up in planning that you don't get out there and do something. You will not know what you need to know until you start. Some obstacles and opportunities will not become visible until you are in the middle of your project.

So get moving! You already have what you need to take the first step. It might not be a big first step—it might be getting a book on your topic from the library or sitting down at your kitchen table with a wise adult, as Joshua did. But that first step will lead you to new resources, new ideas, and a clearer vision that will help you take the next step after that.

I want to obey my parents, and I also want to make my own decisions about the hard things I do. Can those two things go together?

When you first approach your parents with your idea, take them through the process that got you excited. You may want to recruit somebody like a youth pastor or friend of the family to join you in conversation with your parents about what you want to do. This kind of effort will help your parents realize how much you care about the idea.

Keep in mind that your parents might want to see you grow in other areas before you do the hard thing you have in mind. For instance, they might be most concerned with how messy your room is, your attitude when helping with household chores, and the way you interact with your siblings. They might say that you are not ready for a new project until you have made progress in these other areas or shown how you can follow through on a smaller project. There is wisdom (and love) in such an assessment.

Having said that, our family has always operated from the principle that you don't get it together and go—you more often get it together *by* going. In other words, you could make some sort of agreement or contract with your parents that you are going to raise your level of performance in these other areas of your life in order to gain their confidence in your readiness to take steps toward the thing you really want to do. This puts the burden on you to follow through, but it also demonstrates to your family how serious you are about pursuing your vision.

Consider how Michael's story shows a compromise between waiting to do a hard thing and getting started right away:

Right after I read *Do Hard Things*, God led me to start a charity or organization. I call it Operation Reconstruction, or Hands Out. We would help homeless people or unemployed people find a job.

But then my parents suggested I become a teenage cadet in the Civil Air Patrol (CAP) in the Air Force Auxiliary. At first I was against the idea because I thought it would take me away from doing God's will. I tried to persuade my parents to let me start my organization instead. They said no. Then a man of God in our church suggested I list reasons why I should join the Civil Air Patrol and why I shouldn't. Through that exercise, I realized that God's will was for me to do CAP. I believe He is going to use CAP to teach me organization, leadership, and punctuality.

So this is just my first step in doing hard things. I am taking it in faith and not looking back.
—Michael, age 14
Birmingham, Alabama

Michael had the humility to trust that his parents knew what would help him most at this stage in life—and the wisdom to recognize that God was not saying, "No," to his idea for a charity but was saying, "Not yet."

The reality is, no matter how hard you try, your parents might still say no to the hard thing you want to do. Honoring your parents is commanded in Scripture. Odds are that your specific project is not. When in doubt, side with what God makes clear in His Word.

Even when your parents cannot provide you with a satisfactory reason for saying no, you can trust that God is big enough to work through their decision. If God can turn the heart of a king like a stream of water (see Proverbs 21:1), then He can certainly handle your parents.

So be patient with God, because that is really who you are dealing with. And remember that just because you can't set sail for Africa doesn't mean you can't read books or start getting everything in place in case circumstances change.

Your parents might be offering you wise, prayerful counsel that God is using to shepherd you away from a bad decision. Or they might be holding you back from pursuing a great idea you have. Either way, God is not calling you to live in rebellion against them. Your hard thing right now might be to honor your parents' restrictions and prepare your heart and mind for the next hard thing when the time is right.

How do I ask people to support my cause?

We've heard from a lot of rebelutionaries who say the hardest part of their hard thing was working up the courage to talk to people they didn't know—and we've heard from a lot of these same rebelutionaries that talking to others turned out to be a lot easier than they had feared. Often the first phone call or the first time approaching a stranger is the hardest, but each time you make contact with someone, you gain confidence.

As Rachel writes, "God has shown me that I can do what seems to be impossible." She tells us:

Last year I was diagnosed as a type 1 diabetic. Pumps make diabetics' lives much better, but they are quite expensive. I was blessed to get one, and it makes a world of difference in handling my blood sugar and helping me stay healthier. But I couldn't have my own pump without thinking of other kids who don't have one and might need one even more than I did.

So I put together an organization called Loving Actions and decided to host a charity dinner and silent auction to raise money for another diabetic to buy an insulin pump.

The first thing I did was contact my doctor's office, and they supported me every step of the way. They even hooked me up with a family to help. I asked one of my nurses to speak at my dinner and asked a group from my church to sing. I sold tickets and even got on stage and spoke a little bit.

My goal was to raise $3,000, but the turnout was greater than I had expected; the generous donations kept coming even after the dinner was over. I ended up raising $6,590, which was enough to pay for the pump and one year's worth of supplies! The pump and supplies went to an eleven-year-old girl who goes to the same doctor as I do.

I had many doubts in myself because I don't like talking to people I don't know, and I am especially nervous when speaking to adults. God wiped my fears into nonexistence as I just took one step after another.

—Rachel, age 15
Farmington, Arkansas

The exact approach to take when you talk to either friends or strangers depends on what your hard thing is, but the more you know about your project and the more passionate you are about it, the more effective your conversation will be.

Rachel's enthusiasm was catching because the issue was so important to *her*. If you can demonstrate that you are invested in what you are doing, you will motivate others to invest as well.

People are also more willing to help someone they have a positive relationship with. That's why Rachel enlisted the help of a nurse who was familiar with her story and a group of people from her church. They knew her as someone who cared about others, someone they would like to help succeed. As John Maxwell writes in *The 21 Irrefutable Laws of Leadership*, "You first have to touch people's hearts before you can ask them for a hand."[3]

You also want to be creative with how you develop and name your project. Joshua Guthrie, for example, found a "hook" that helped him approach people about the well in Sudan without having to explain a lot. He did a lot of planning, but the idea itself was simple: a dollar for a drink. The name of his organization described what he was asking people to do. It was catchy, intriguing, and simple. He also had a website to which he could direct people for more information.

Keep in mind that whenever you are trying to recruit people to support your cause or project, you run the risk of coming across as someone who is only interested in what other people can do for you. Instead, ask yourself, *How could my project work as a vehicle for their aspirations and interests?* When Rachel asked herself this, she turned to her doctor's office and to another family who could benefit from her fund-raiser.

When we were just starting our blog, we became friends with a more established blogger by promoting something she was doing and then, at her request, using our high-school debate experience to write blog-commenting guidelines for her heavily trafficked blog. Out of gratitude—and without our asking—she put up a permanent link to our blog on her website and later wrote a newspaper article about what we were doing.

Just as doing hard things involves using your gifts, getting other people involved means being aware of their gifts. With this change in perspective, instead of going into a conversation thinking you know how a person is going to help you, you will be ready to engage the person about what he or she is able and eager to do.

What are some ideas for getting my church to participate?

Just like any individual, a church as an institution has goals and interests that your project can serve. Your youth pastor has certain things he wants to accomplish in the lives of the young people in his care. Your pastor may be interested in raising the church's profile in the community. Everyone (we hope) will be interested in furthering the gospel and building up the body of Christ. The more you understand these dynamics, the better you will be able to serve your church through your project.

Kyrstin's story reminds us that serving the church, like all hard things, starts with a change in attitude.

After my family moved from Maine to Arkansas, it was
hard to find a home church. I felt lonely, overwhelmed,
and discouraged about our new life. Then it hit me. I had

been looking for my pleasure, my church, and my life.
I needed to look beyond my selfish perspective and ask,
Where does God want me to serve?

We did find a church—a hurting church with many
areas in which my family could serve. From the second
time I attended my new youth group, I found out why
God had sent me there.

Our church has a Korean church inside it, and the
Korean teens attend our youth group. The first time I went
to youth group, I saw a distinct line between the American
teens and the Korean teens. Most of it was just a language
barrier. So the second time I attended, I decided I was
going to meet some of the Koreans and try to break down
the walls between us.

Thankfully, God stepped in for a shy girl like me,
and some of the Korean girls approached me first. For the
weeks following that meeting, I continued to sit with these
girls during the Bible lesson and helped them understand
the American games we played. I became closer to them
than I was to any of the other teens who went there.

Then, soon after getting involved with the Korean-
American youth group, I found out that a person at my
dad's work was looking for someone to teach a friend con-
versational English. I quickly agreed and found myself
with yet another Korean friend and a lot of great teaching
experience.

Little did I know that one attitude change about
church was just the beginning of doing hard things! But
God knew. I guess that shows how important—no matter
what the size—hard things are. Yes, it's hard, but it's

drawing you to be more like Jesus, so it's worth it. And
compared to what I ended up doing, the hard things I'd
had in mind were quite dinky!
    —Kyrstin, age 19
    Little Rock, Arkansas

Are you asking yourself, *What can I get out of this church to help
me?* Or are you asking, *How can I serve my church through doing this
hard thing?* As our dad has always told us, we do well for ourselves by doing good for others. Be open to how *you* can help
your church, rather than the other way around. This change in
Kyrstin's perspective opened her eyes to the needs of the girls in
her youth group and led to other opportunities she hadn't even
known existed.

If your hard thing involves first communicating with your
pastor, don't pitch your idea as another thing for him to do but
as something *you* want to help make happen for the good of the
church he cares about. If speaking to your youth pastor, make it
clear that you want this to be a student-led project. Few youth
pastors will turn down a good idea that doesn't require extra
work on their part and provides students with an opportunity to
grow and work together.

Remember that if you want to get your church involved in a
particular project, check the calendar. Most churches have full
schedules of ministry events they have committed to—sometimes
a year in advance. If you are ignorant of their schedule or just
impatient and end up competing with something already on the
calendar, you will have trouble getting any support from the
church leadership.

Of course, it will be difficult to convince your youth pastor or pastor to get behind something you are doing if you aren't already involved in your church. It will come across that you don't care about the church except when it can help you do something you want to do. So if you don't participate because you disagree with the way things are done, then communicate your concerns and share that you want to be part of the solution by putting time and energy into an alternative. But if there are already good things happening in your church that you don't take the time to support, get involved and start from there.

Kyrstin jumped in to what her church was already doing—building a bridge between Korean teens and American teens. If a specific opportunity like that doesn't come to mind, think on a very practical level. Could you help set up chairs before the service? Offer to mow the lawn, clean up after a potluck, or vacuum the Sunday school rooms?

The most important thing is to show up. Participate in youth activities. Attend services. Becoming a thriving and contributing member of your local church is vitally important, regardless of whether you have a specific ministry project to pitch. (This helps us remember that the house of God is not a glorified networking opportunity!) We will prosper as we help God's church to prosper. And when we are connected with other believers, it will not be long before kingdom partnerships start taking place.

I'm not big on bake sales. How can I raise money for my project?

First, don't write off bake sales. Even if baking isn't your thing, see if you can get your mom (and your friends) to help out. Who doesn't like homemade cookies, pie, or cake? Second, with a little creativity, there are hundreds of ways to raise money for your project. Here are a few examples to help get you started:

- Turn your bake sale into a fast-paced auction at your church or school—and sell Aunt Martha's famous gooey chocolate cake to the highest bidder.
- Host a silent auction at your church, and have people bid on paper. Don't forget you can sell time or talent: two hours of baby-sitting or yard work, one private violin concert during dinner, tax advice from your accountant dad (get his okay on this one first!), homework help for an elementary schooler. This is a great way to raise money *and* match up the needs and gifts of people in your church.
- Host a pancake breakfast for your community. Sell tickets at the door, and have a donation tin as people leave. You can have different rates for adults, kids, and families. Ask local stores and restaurants to donate food.
- Do a movie night at your local park or gymnasium. Set up a screen and projector, show a classic, and sell popcorn and soda.
- Organize a walkathon, marathon, or 5K race. Have participants get friends and family to sponsor them by pledging money. Ask local businesses to donate prizes— both for the winners and the top fund-raisers.
- Reach out to churches in your area, and ask if you can come and talk to their congregation about your project. If they are supportive, ask if they'd be willing to take a special offering for your cause.

- Design and make T-shirts, silicone bracelets, or other items that can be sold to raise money for your cause. If they look cool and support a great cause, people will be glad to donate—and they'll be walking billboards for your project!

These are just a few ideas. Almost all of them can be tweaked for your situation. Baked goods can be replaced with handmade crafts; a pancake breakfast can become a soup-and-salad supper; a movie night can morph into a live music concert; a walkathon can become a stand-a-thon, jump-a-thon, or anything-else-a-thon.

Be creative! And remember to use each of these fund-raisers as an opportunity to educate your community about your cause. You'll be surprised by how supportive people will be when they're getting something good for themselves (like a pie, a pancake, a movie, a run, or a nifty bracelet) *and* supporting a cause they believe is important.

How can I get my friends involved in a group effort?

Fifteen-year-old Hali Hilts first heard about the chocolate slave trade from a speaker at her school. As she looked into human trafficking more, she found out that the majority of the chocolate she and her friends (and most of us) eat is produced by slaves—often young boys who are abused.

"It's rarely talked about because it's so widely done," she tells us. "I didn't know how I could make a difference in such an overwhelming problem or how I could get anyone else interested. I decided to first make a change in my own life. Maybe that would inspire others. So I started eating only fair-trade chocolate—chocolate that is produced in an ethical way."

Hali's simple choice means she often has to turn down her favorite foods at social events. "My friends started asking me why I wasn't eating chocolate much anymore," she says. "That gave me the opportunity to tell people about it. Now a lot of my friends are only eating fair-trade chocolate. We are raising awareness in our community and starting to work on a website and a pamphlet. It's a practical thing. That's why I like it."

The best thing you can do to get your peers excited about your hard thing is to retrace your own steps. What first got *you* excited about your project?

If you read a book or watched a video online and suddenly became concerned about human trafficking, then share that book or video with your friends. Whatever lit your fuse may light their fuses as well.

Tell your friends how your new knowledge or idea has changed you. Just as Hali did, show your friends that *you* are willing to make sacrifices before asking them to do the same.

Another way to recruit your friends is to just ask them. "Wouldn't you like to make something happen instead of just watching something happen? Wouldn't you like to be a producer rather than a consumer?" The world is full of people whose lives are boring and empty. Some of your friends might fall into this category—they might welcome a vision of living with deeper purpose.

After all, hanging out at the mall together is great, but it cannot compare to putting your hands to the same cause. And people who work together the best also play together the best. You'll have a new level of friendship and camaraderie when you work hard toward a common goal and then go out for pizza.

Along the way, you might discover secret rebelutionaries.

These are the young people around you whose hearts are silently crying out, *God has bigger plans for me than this. There's more to me than what this culture expects.*

Your mission: find these people! They probably won't reveal themselves until you reveal yourself. You may have to do your initial hard things alone. But if you start living as if the idea of adolescence is a lie and start doing hard things, you'll attract the secret rebelutionaries who just needed to hear the battle cry and see a fellow soldier running into the battle.

As Esther discovered, they might pick up their weapons and start running too.

There it was again, staring me down. A heinous image painted on canvas and now hung silently on the wall. In its silence, it said a thousand things.

I lowered my gaze and thought about the rest of the sexual images displayed as "artwork" around school. I wanted to do something. I thought about sending a petition around to my group of friends. If we got enough signatures as a complaint, the paintings might be taken down.

I suggested the petition to a group of friends. I was not alone in my opinion.

"I'll be the first to sign it!" one boy exclaimed. Several people nodded and said they were with me on the project. Then my friend spoke up.

"I'm so with you on this one! If you bring in the petition, I'll go with you to make the complaint, and I'll take it to all my classes and have people sign it." While I was very glad for the backup, something inside me hesitated.

I wanted credit for taking a stand. I was being the
Gideon here, the Lone Ranger. Not her. Then I realized
that the object was not to climb some mountain of greatness or get my name on a plaque. The goal was to remove
the things that cause people to stumble in their walk with
God.

"Besides," God reminded me, "If you're going to be a
true Gideon, you'll need about three hundred buddies to
help you."

The next day, I brought in the petition, ready for signatures. They came in steadily, and as they did, I began
to appreciate my outspoken friend more. Outgoing and
friendly, she presented the petition to many people, nearly
always coming back with more signatures. The more people we had working toward a common goal, the closer the
goal became.

The petition will be turned in tomorrow, and my
friends and I wait, praying that it will be recognized.
Whether it is or isn't, I know we have made our voices
heard. We fought to defend Christ's name, and now it's up
to God. I know that God has before and will again use the
faith of a group of people—even a group of high-school
kids.

—Esther, age 18
Medway, Ohio

"If you're going to be a true Gideon, you'll need about three
hundred buddies to help you." What a great way to describe how
we rely on each other in doing hard things!

If and when a group of friends takes shape around your

project, remember that the person who provides the catalyst for bringing people together and setting a vision is not necessarily the best person to lead the project on a daily basis. Have the humility to assess whether you are the one to lead the project long-term. You will probably want to get feedback from others about this. It also takes humility to distinguish between friends who aren't excited about working on a particular project and friends who aren't excited about working with you because of certain attitudes and tendencies you need to change.

If your friends don't respond as enthusiastically as the secret rebelutionaries around Esther did, use technology to find people who share your passion, and through working together, make new friends. For every issue that excites you, you can probably find numerous blogs, discussion boards, and online groups of fellow enthusiasts.[4]

Finally: let go. While you might think everyone should care about your specific cause or project, God doesn't place the same calling on every person's heart. Don't judge others because they aren't as excited as you are. Give them the freedom to work out their own story with God in His time.

SIDE EFFECTS MAY OCCUR

Handling the changes that come with doing hard things

Ever gotten a big compliment from someone (usually an adult) who's amazed that a teenager is doing something that actually matters? We have. And so have a lot of other rebelutionaries. One of our friends described the feeling well.

"I don't deserve all this praise, and it makes me feel uncomfortable," she tells us. "It must grieve the Lord that so little is expected of His children."

You already know that your *attitude* changes when you do hard things. What can sometimes come as a surprise is how your *outer* life changes too—what people say to you, how you use your time, and even the "celebrity" status that can come with accomplishing something meaningful.

When we started the Rebelution, we weren't looking to start a movement or an organization. We didn't plan to put on conferences, give interviews, or write a book. We certainly didn't expect to be recognized by complete strangers or to have people ask us for our autographs.

Our lives have changed a lot in the last few years, in big and small ways. It's been strange, exciting, and *very hard*. With attention comes criticism—both valid and not. Traveling, or even just being busy, makes it harder to spend time with friends and maintain relationships. Thankfully, to our family and close friends, we're still just Alex and Brett. They help keep us grounded when we're feeling up and help us up when we're feeling down. They remind us that it is both exciting and humbling to be involved in what God is doing in our generation.

All of the questions in this chapter are ones we've asked ourselves at different points. As God has blessed the work of the Rebelution, we've had to figure out how to deal with affirmation, fight pride, do media interviews, and manage our time.

If God is calling you to walk a similar path, we hope this chapter will prepare you for the blessings and challenges to come.

What's the best way to handle the affirmation I receive for doing hard things?

Few rebelutionaries receive the attention that Zac Sunderland has. At the age of sixteen, he took the money he'd earned from summer jobs and bought a thirty-six-foot sailboat. He named his boat *Intrepid*. Zac surprised even his parents with the scope of his dream: to circumnavigate the globe by himself. As a teenager.

On July 16, 2009, Zac sailed the *Intrepid* into Marina del Rey, California, after thirteen months alone at sea. Zac broke the record for the youngest person in history to sail solo around the world—the first under the age of eighteen to do so.

It's hard to describe just how much work this was. Zac spent eighteen-hour days getting the *Intrepid* ready to sail. During his journey, he battled storms, illness, pirates, loneliness, and fear. He was away from his family for more than a year.

When asked what inspired him, Zac tells us, "Society puts younger people...in kind of a box, no one's really expected to do much. There's so much more potential that people can do with the right motivation and the right ambition in life. So my thing would just be to get out there and do hard things. Go for it."[1]

But when Zac returned home, he faced a different kind of challenge: a bigger media frenzy and more personal affirmation than he'd ever experienced before. He even made the cover of *ESPN The Magazine*, with an article titled "Do Hard Things"— inspired by a T-shirt he wore on his incredible journey, emblazoned with the rebelutionary motto.

We asked Zac what it was like to be such a high-profile rebelutionary. How did he stay humble in the midst of television interviews and magazine covers? What would he say to other rebelutionaries attracting attention for doing hard things— sometimes *a lot* of attention? This is what he said:

Having a lot of media attention can be really exciting and a bit overwhelming, but it can get old pretty fast. My advice would be to keep a level head, and remember the message you're trying to get across. Surrounding yourself with godly people is key to doing this. For example, my publicist is a Christian and has been great at counseling me before public appearances. I have a few Christian friends who are high-profile people, and it has been great to have them around to share their experience and wisdom. They have seen a lot of people take the wrong path and reap the consequences.

I think that it helps not to have fame as your goal. My goal was to have an adventure and see the world, and that is who I am and always have been.[2]

There's nothing wrong with receiving attention or gaining a platform. Both are gifts from God. Attention gives us the opportunity to humbly say thanks and then point people back to the One who made us, sustains us, and gives us everything we have (see Colossians 1:15–20). It also gives us the opportunity to tell people our true goal, as Zac has done.

God calls some people to be *faithful and content* even if no one knows their names. We will probably all be surprised when we get to heaven and see who has the biggest crowns to lay at Jesus' feet. It won't be the famous but rather the quiet faithful—those who served, prayed, and labored in relative obscurity.

But God also calls some of us to be *faithful and humble* in the limelight. If He chooses to give us attention, then we are responsible to use it for His glory.

This can be one of the most difficult parts of doing hard things. As Proverbs 27:21 tells us, "The crucible for silver and the furnace for gold, but man is tested by the praise he receives" (NIV).

In our own lives, as the Rebelution took off and our profile began to rise, people began to say nice things about us. Some people said very nice things.

We still remember the day we received Randy Alcorn's endorsement for *Do Hard Things*. Randy is one of our modern-day heroes, a best-selling author, and an old family friend. We knew he wouldn't write an endorsement unless he really believed in the book.

Needless to say, we were blown away when we received his extremely positive endorsement via e-mail. We were overwhelmed with gratitude for his kind words but even more grateful for how he closed his e-mail, with the following charge:

> I encourage you to consciously pursue humility and not
> allow Satan to get an inroad in your lives with the praise
> you will be receiving for this book. Deflect that praise to
> Christ, not to appear humble, but to be humble. You are
> chosen by God, and also targeted by Satan. Humble your-
> selves and God will lift you up. He opposes the proud and
> gives grace to the humble. Do not succumb to pride, realiz-
> ing to do so is to put yourself under God's opposition.[3]

After reading Randy's e-mail, we immediately fell on our faces on the floor (literally) and cried out to God to give us a spirit of humility. We've found that our sinful hearts will take every opportunity to cultivate pride. And nothing is more dangerous to our souls or the long-term future of the work we are doing than to give in to that pride.

Along the way, we have identified two types of pride that we must battle continually.

The First Type of Pride

The first type of pride is the temptation to take credit for the things God has done through us. We have found, though, that this expression of pride dies when confronted with our absolute dependency on God. Here are a few verses that put this into perspective:

- Psalm 16:2: "You are my Lord; I have no good apart from you."
- James 1:17: "Every good gift and every perfect gift is from above" (NIV).
- John 3:27: "A person cannot receive *even one thing* unless it is given him from heaven."
- Isaiah 26:12: "You have indeed done for us all our works."

In his book *David: Man of Prayer, Man of War,* Walter Chantry has written one of the most helpful things we've read on this topic. Commenting on the verse "The LORD gave victory to David wherever he went" (2 Samuel 8:14), Chantry writes:

All of David's successful conquests are explained in this way: "The LORD gave victory to David wherever he went." Again we discover that the history of David is not about what David did for God, but about what God did for David!

The grace of God for man is too often turned into the idea that it is man who does heroic feats for God. Our humanistic dream is that we may do great things for God. We shall give our genius, our talents, and our strength to him.... Yet the theme of grace is what he does for us!

The Almighty is not in a tight spot, needing men to come to his rescue. It is we who, in every hour and emergency of life, stand in need of the Lord to uphold and to deliver us. It is tragic when readers of Scripture barely notice the historical record, "The LORD gave victory to

David," but rather bolster their humanistic theory that
"David surely gave the Lord's cause a boost in his day."[4]

Rather than thinking we are "giving God a boost" through
the work He equips us to do, we can thank Him for including us
in what He is doing. He doesn't need us, but He works through
us for our good and His glory.

The Second Type of Pride

The second type of pride is more difficult to fight: the pride of
enjoying praise, expecting praise, and being disappointed when
others don't appreciate us the way we think they should. This
kind of pride is common among those of us who have learned to
avoid more blatant expressions of arrogance.

Only God's opinion matters. As eighteenth-century evangel-
ist George Whitefield—a star in his day—wrote, "Lord, lead me
through this fight. Help me see the vanity of all commendation
but Thine own." If God approves, then no other affirmation is necessary. If He does not approve, then who cares if the whole world
cheers?

When Zac Sunderland pulled into the harbor after his thirteen
months at sea, he faced a choice—the same choice any of us faces
when someone speaks well of us. He could take all the credit. He
could put himself down, as if he hadn't just sailed around the
world. Or he could do what he did: acknowledge the truth of what
he accomplished and acknowledge that it was God who helped
him accomplish it. Now he is using his platform to challenge teens
to do more than society expects—and giving the glory to God.

It can be uncomfortable when people praise us for doing

hard things, especially because that praise is often the result of low expectations in the first place. Nevertheless, when we're praised publicly, we have an opportunity to set an example for others (like 1 Timothy 4:12 says). We can point out that we're just doing what we're supposed to be doing.

This is how the Rebelution movement will continue to grow—as ordinary teens use the attention they receive for doing hard things to bust the Myth of Adolescence and spread a biblical view of the teen years.

Like every gift from God, affirmation is something we can recognize and enjoy as long as we remember its source. Holocaust survivor and author Corrie ten Boom is quoted as saying, "When people come up and give me a compliment—'Corrie, that was a good talk,' or 'Corrie, you were so brave,' I take each remark as if it were a flower. At the end of each day I lift up the bouquet of flowers I have gathered throughout the day and say, 'Here you are, Lord, it is all yours.'"[5]

My dream is bigger than my schedule! How do I manage my time now that I'm a rebelutionary?

Whether we are committing to spend thirteen months at sea, like Zac did, or tackling a somewhat shorter-term project, all of us have questions about how much time to invest in the dream we want to pursue—and still keep up with our other God-given obligations.

Over the past few years, we have needed to remind ourselves constantly of the difference between busyness (having a lot to do) and fruitfulness (accomplishing something of eternal significance).

This realization first struck us as we read a blog series by C. J. Mahaney on the topic of biblical productivity. In the opening post, he writes:

> Lazy? Not me. I'm busy. Up early, up late. My schedule is filled from beginning to end. I love what I do and I love getting stuff done. I attack a daily to-do list with the same intensity I play basketball. Me lazy? I don't think so!
>
> Or at least I didn't think so. That is, until I read about the difference between busyness and fruitfulness, and realized just how often my busyness was an expression of laziness, not diligence.
>
> I forget now who first brought these points to my attention. But the realization that I could be simultaneously busy and lazy, that I could be a hectic sluggard, that my busyness was no immunity from laziness, became a life-altering and work-altering insight. What I learned is that:
>
> > Busyness does not mean I am *diligent*.
> > Busyness does not mean I am *faithful*.
> > Busyness does not mean I am *fruitful*.
>
> Recognizing the sin of procrastination, and broadening the definition to include busyness, has made a significant alteration in my life. The sluggard can be busy—busy neglecting the most important work, and busy knocking out a to-do list filled with tasks of secondary importance.[6]

If you are a busy person, ask yourself, *What kind of busy am I?* Are you intentionally busy, with purposeful, fruitful work? Or are you busy in the sense that you're always doing something, don't have any extra time during the day, and feel tired and irritated a lot?

We've found that bad sleep habits and mindless web surfing can make us feel busy but actually drain our productivity. When we're staying up late, we get less quantity and quality of sleep. We've been surprised by how much more productive we are (and how much better we feel) when we get enough sleep and wake up earlier. We've also found that if we're not careful, we can easily waste hours and hours of time online. Being disciplined and organized in how we use our time is one of those important small hard things that allows us to do some of the bigger hard things God's given us to do.

Even *good* activities might not be the *best* activities for a particular season of life. If you're anything like us, you find it difficult to say no. Every invitation is exciting, every request appealing, every opportunity "once in a lifetime." As you may have already discovered, the more you do, the more people ask you to do. It's a compliment, but it isn't always compatible with your schedule.

But how do you say no? Doesn't the fact that God presented you with the opportunity mean you're supposed to take it?

As we were wrestling with these questions a few years ago, we had an opportunity to talk again with our good friend and mentor Randy Alcorn. We explained to him our dilemma. How should we decide which speaking invitations to accept? How do we know which projects to pursue?

With wisdom gained over decades of wrestling with the same questions, Randy told us:

I've learned I need to say no to the majority of good opportunities, and even to some great ones, in order to be free to
say yes to those very few things God has equipped and
called me to do.

I used to think that if I said no to something, it was
saying no to God. I came to realize that by saying yes to
many things people wanted me to do, I was putting myself
in a position where I was saying no to God. Or even when
I said yes, I didn't have the time and energy to do the best
job at what He really wanted me to do.[7]

Randy's advice was encouraging, comforting, and helpful.
We realized that we didn't have to do everything and be every-
where in order to serve God. We actually make ourselves *more*
fruitful when we learn to say no (and yes) to the right things.

One of the important things we know God has called us to is
to attend college. Being full-time students has led us to say no to
a lot of good opportunities. But saying no doesn't stress us out
the way it used to. We know that we're being responsible by
investing the appropriate amount of time and energy into our
long-term preparation.

Hannah's story is a good example of choosing to spend time
on long-term goals even when it means sacrificing short-term
opportunities:

Getting an A in my first dual-credit college class wasn't
easy. It took keeping track of assignments and editing my
papers, watching a video on government that wasn't nearly
as exciting as anything I would watch on my own, and
debating my beliefs. It took biking four miles each way to

get to school, even if fog hung low or dense rain slicked the road.

Even though I was the only high schooler in the class of college students, my teacher realized that I was not like the teenagers he knew. I realized how much everything I do is a representation of my entire age group and that I have a responsibility to give adults a reason to not look down on young people.

When my class load increases as I graduate high school, I will be well prepared to work and attend college at the same time. I know how to handle my time better, and I am on my way to meeting my goal of graduating college early.

I'll admit that I do get overwhelmed sometimes, but feeling overwhelmed only teaches me to rely more on God. I've also come to realize that it's important not to be out there on my own. God brings people into my life for a reason, and they have helped me through a lot. Sometimes all I need to know is that someone else cares about what I'm going through.

If I feel too overwhelmed about doing hard things in life, I remember that courage is about choosing to try again the next day and the next. God can give me that courage.

—Hannah, age 18
Los Banos, California

It takes *courage* to manage time well—and to invest time well—because it takes courage to say yes or no to opportunities based on God's direction rather than on our culture's assumptions.

Are you saying yes because you want to look good or you don't want someone else to get the credit? Are you saying no because you are fearful or because you procrastinated so much on other obligations that now you don't have time for this one? Or are you saying yes because you believe that God is calling you to this new thing? Are you saying no because you need to free up time to do your best in the areas God *has* called you to?

Many of the suggestions we made in chapter 2 about how to choose what hard thing to do still apply once we start doing hard things. We need to keep asking good questions about our time, our priorities, and our goals, always remembering that *God does not give us conflicting obligations.*

In our own lives, having seemingly too much to do can actually make us more productive. It forces us to be purposeful in our use of time and to cut out unimportant things. Like Hannah, we've found that stretching ourselves requires us to rely on God in order to get everything done. We try to keep our schedule right outside our comfort zone, but not in the danger zone, where the quality of our work, important relationships, or obligations suffer.

As we seek to honor God and push ourselves, we've also found that setting aside Sabbath time is one of the best ways to keep godly priorities in our lives. Intentionally "wasting time with God"—whether in praying, taking a walk, reading, even sleeping—can remind us of the paradox that we are called to do great work and yet the world is not on our shoulders.

Spending time alone with God can help us distinguish between busyness and fruitfulness. As Dallas Willard writes:

> Solitude well practiced will break the power of busyness, haste, isolation and loneliness.... You will find yourself and God will find you in new ways. Joy and peace will begin to bubble up within you and arrive from things and events

around you. Praise and prayer will come to you and from within you. The soul anchor established in solitude will remain solid when you return to your ordinary life with others.[8]

The best way to remember God's calling in all our decisions is to know God more. When we set aside time—whether on a Sunday or another day, whether in the morning or late at night—to simply be with God and not "do" anything for Him, we become better equipped to serve Him.

What should I do when people want to interview me?

Talking "in front" of people—whether in a group, for the newspaper, on the radio, or even on TV—can be one of the hardest, scariest things you'll ever do. But it can also be one of the best opportunities to give glory to God and correct the lies our culture believes about the teen years.

When we started doing interviews for the Rebelution and *Do Hard Things*, we first talked through what we needed to communicate. We often wrote down key phrases and lines we wanted to make sure we got right. Then we practiced them so they didn't sound scripted. We also got a feel for the person interviewing us by watching or listening to or reading other interviews he or she had done.

Keep in mind that the person interviewing you might know very little about you, what you've written, or what you've done. That's just part of working with media. Your interviewer may or may not be a Christian. He or she may even be antagonistic toward Christianity. That's one of the reasons it helps to have in mind ahead of time what you want to say—it frees you to speak truth in love and make your point well, not get into an argument.

Also remember that although you want to respect an interviewer's questions, you can always use a question as a launching pad to discuss a key point you want to make—even if it's not an exact answer to the question just asked.

It helps to think of an interview as an *intentional conversation* rather than a strict Q and A. What do you most want someone to know about you or your project? If you are preparing for an interview, you might want to have a family member or friend help you practice by asking you questions.

Especially at first, it's good to err on the side of being over-prepared. The irony is that the more you prepare, the more natural you can feel in the actual interview.

One danger when you do an interview is that whenever a young person has done something commendable, our culture wants to praise you as an individual exception. The sinful tendency is to get comfortable with this "one of a kind" status and take the glory of our accomplishments for ourselves.

We are called by God to be examples, not exceptions. The message of the Rebelution is that all young people have the ability to accomplish far greater things than our culture would have them think. We live a different way to show our culture a better way.

Just like any other ability, doing interviews is something that gets easier with practice. Interviews can provide great opportunities to turn the focus from ourselves as individuals to the growing ranks of ordinary teens who are turning low expectations on their head—and to the God who strengthens them to do it.

MATTERS OF FIRST IMPORTANCE

Keeping God in focus every step of the way

As the Rebelution has grown, the two of us have gotten busier and busier with traveling, speaking, writing, and now college. We've also gotten more attention—some of it very flattering, some of it very critical. All of those things make it easy to get our focus off God and on ourselves or our immediate circumstances. It's a constant struggle.

As we saw in the previous chapter, getting attention is not inherently wrong—and it can be used for much good. Our reasons for seeking attention and the way we respond to it *can* be dishonoring to Christ. But on the flip side, doing hard things for Christ is one of the primary ways we can glorify Him.

Why is that? Because if we restrict ourselves to what comes easily, avoid sacrifices, and limit our relationship with God to Sunday mornings, we're showing the world how little we value Him. When we're willing to take risks, pursue excellence, dream big, be faithful, and do what's right no matter the cost, our actions shout that Christ is worth serving above all others.

In this chapter we'll explore both principles and practical steps for integrating our rebelutionary lifestyle with the meaning and purpose of our lives as God's children.

I want God to be at the center of every hard thing I do. What does that look like?

At times we're all guilty of thinking of God as more like a big cosmic riddle than what He really is—a person. Granted, He's a perfect, infinite, all-wise, and all-powerful person, but He's a person nonetheless.

When we forget that God is a person, we ask questions we'd never think twice about if we were talking about our best friend or someone we love. This question is a good example of that. When we think about what it looks like to make God the most important thing in our lives, we get confused. But how would we answer that question if we were talking about another person—someone we admired and respected more than anyone else?

We'd want to know everything about him—his likes and dislikes, what makes him happy, what makes him sad. Nothing would seem too insignificant to us.

We'd want to find out what he thought about things. His opinion would be more influential than everyone else's combined.

We'd want to learn what he loves, and we would come to love the same things.

As we went through our day-to-day lives, he would be on our minds. As we made decisions about what to wear, what to buy, and how to spend our time, we'd think about what he would do. We'd make decisions we believed would please him.

We wouldn't just try to fit him into our lifestyle and schedule. Instead, we'd look forward to experiencing life with him. We would make changes in our schedule so we could spend more time together. We would be honored if he asked us to be part of what he was doing. In fact, we would drop what we were working on to join him in his work.

Because we admire him, we would want people to identify us with him. We would want to represent him accurately so other people would get to know him as well.

Doesn't this seem like a natural response to liking and admiring someone? Of course, the catch is that if we go to the extreme in treating a human friend like this, we're in danger of idolizing him. But this *is* how we're supposed to relate to God. It's how we bring Him glory as we do hard things.

Eli's story gives us a glimpse of what it looks like to put God's thoughts, opinions, and ways before any other person's:

I am a youth minister and a senior studying biochemistry at a small state college. One of my classes required students to design and execute an experiment. A partner and I came up with a great experiment that involved catching fish in different streams, dissecting them, and looking at parasites to see how they relate to fish in other streams. We did this in the winter. We got snowed on several times traveling up and down cold streams with a heavy net, catching fish. It was a wearying job.

We initially wanted fish from five different streams, but we recovered fish from only three. This was bad for our data. My partner wanted to make up figures for a fourth stream so it didn't look so bad. I kept telling him that I didn't think that was a great idea.

Finally I sent him an e-mail saying that I would write my own paper with the correct results. I got a call from him and was cursed at for well over half an hour, but I never caved. I kept telling him that if we are faithful with little, we will be faithful with much. He accused me of all kinds of stuff, but in the end, together, we turned in the true results.

—Eli, age 23
Auburn, Nebraska

Putting God at the center of our lives means caring more about what He thinks than about what other people think—even when their voices, like that of Eli's partner, seem louder than God's.

Putting God at the center of our lives means allowing *Christ in us* to show, whether that means speaking kindly when it would be easier to curse or living with integrity when it would be easier to cheat. We are free to treat others with love, patience, and humility because we are simply reflecting the qualities of a good God—a God who can take sinners and teach them to love one another.

Putting God at the center of our lives means acknowledging our dependence on Him as we do hard things—even when it's tempting to take the credit for ourselves.

Putting God at the center of our lives does not mean we live perfectly. It means we live intentionally. And it will cost us something—whether it's time, money, popularity, personal comfort, or a better grade. It may displace something (or someone) else that is at the center of our lives right now.

In the Bible, God says, "I, the LORD your God, am a jealous God" (Exodus 20:5, NIV). *Jealousy* tends to have negative connotations today, so it can be hard to understand what God meant when He said this to the Israelites. But jealousy in this context is beautiful.

One commentator writes that God's jealousy is His "holy zeal for the honor of his name and the good of his people."[1] God wants what is best for us. And what is best for us is Him!

When we understand this, putting God at the center of our lives is not a vague act of obedience. It is the only sensible response—to Someone we need and long to know more.

How do I keep my motivation for doing hard things pure?

We probably don't need to tell you all the wrong motives a person can have when doing hard things. We know them ourselves: pride, attention, popularity, money, the desire to "impress" God or somehow make Him love us more, wanting our parents to give us more responsibility, or even wanting the admiration of our fellow rebelutionaries.

Pride is such a common temptation that it's a good idea to frequently ask yourself (or ask a mentor to ask you), *Is the way I'm thinking or talking about this hard thing focused on me and my abilities, or is it focused on God—obeying Him and serving others?* One way to catch pride is to watch how we relate to others—or even better, to ask other people to share how we're coming across to them. Are we grasping for praise? Or are we eager to share the credit with those we're working with?

We've found that pride most often creeps in at the beginning
and the end of doing a hard thing. In the middle of doing a hard
thing—when elements are taking longer than we'd planned,
when we're immersed in the details, when others are questioning
whether we'll finish—it's a lot easier to acknowledge how much
we need God! But in the excitement of a new idea or a job well
done, taking pride in our accomplishment rather than God's
accomplishment is very tempting.

We've also found that the amount of praise we get often
doesn't have anything to do with how hard the thing actually
was. In a culture of low expectations, we can be praised for
"doing hard things" without ever really pushing ourselves!

That's why one good way to keep our motivations pure as
we're doing hard things is to keep up with the small hard things—
those difficult daily choices that rarely bring recognition.

The hardest thing for me about doing small things is that
no one notices. I like to be noticed, and I forget that God
does notice and it doesn't matter what the world thinks.

For instance, I sing on my church's worship team.
When people see me in the fellowship hall, they recognize
me and sometimes compliment me. So how can I sing in
front of an audience of 150 when I can barely get my alge-
bra down the hole sometimes? When I am ready to tear
out the hair of certain younger siblings at any given
moment? Perhaps because I'm the only one who knows
whether I finish my schoolwork every day. Perhaps because there's no big audience when I'm patient or impatient with my siblings. Besides, everyone already thinks
that I'm a nice, hard-working person ("Oh, you have such

a nice family!" "Oh, you are such a sweet girl!"). It's easy to just enjoy the reputation without doing the work at home, where no one sees.

The more I think I will change "one of these days," the deeper and deeper I dig the pit. And "one of these days," it will consume me.

Just because I'm writing this doesn't mean that "I'm all fixed up" yet. But I have to keep trying, or I'll let those failures overwhelm me and I'll give up trying at all.

Doing hard things doesn't mean getting seen on TV for all the wonderful things I'm doing. It means glorifying God to the best of my ability in quiet and in public. And trying won't do me any good if I don't let Jesus fight for me, which I know He will do.

—Meg, age 14

Cologne, Germany

Meg speaks for most of us in saying that the hardest hard things to do are the ones no one notices. Those also might be the most important ones to do because they reveal our true character—and keep our motivations in check.

So here you are: you want to do something hard for the glory of God, but you also wouldn't mind your pastor praising you in front of church, your dad acknowledging that you did what he didn't think you could do, or your older sister being out of the spotlight for once. Should you not do the hard thing?

If we wait for perfectly pure motives, we will never do anything. As Meg says, we will keep waiting for "one of these days." But we *can* pray for God to alert us when our motives are impure. We *can* pray for wisdom in choosing hard things for the right reason. God honors our desire to obey Him and become more like Him. He *wants* to refine our motives, and He is patient to do that.

When we do recognize our mixed motivations, our prayer might be simple: "God, I confess I am caring more about what my professor thinks of me right now than about whether You are pleased. Forgive me. Help me to keep going for the right reasons. Amen."

And just like Meg, we keep going. If we dwell on our motives too much, we will be distracted. If we keep putting ourselves down for our sinfulness, we will be so focused on ourselves that we'll have a kind of reverse pride and *still* not be focused on God or others.

This is not to say that our motivations don't matter to God. As Paul says in Romans:

> What then? Shall we sin because we are not under law but under grace? By no means! Don't you know that when you offer yourselves to someone to obey him as slaves, you are slaves to the one whom you obey—whether you are slaves to sin, which leads to death, or to obedience, which leads to righteousness?... You have been set free from sin and have become slaves to righteousness. (Romans 6:15–16, 18, NIV)

Pride might be a part of your life, but you are not a slave to pride. Sin—the wrong motivations—"shall not be your master, because you are not under law, but under grace" (Romans 6:14, NIV). In Meg's words, failure does not need to overwhelm you because Jesus is still fighting for you.

When God prompts you to recognize sin in your life, put it in its place—under the grace of God, where it cannot motivate you *or* keep you from doing hard things.

Sometimes doing hard things actually distracts me from God. What should I do?

If we're doing the wrong things for the wrong reasons, we shouldn't be surprised when they start undermining other aspects of our lives. But what about good hard things? What if you're working to raise money for orphans in Cambodia, planning an evangelism outreach concert at your local park, or working your first job—and your relationship with God starts to suffer?

We know the feeling. When we interned at the Alabama Supreme Court, one of the hardest things (and one we didn't do perfectly) was establishing good devotional habits. We knew we didn't have to pray and read our Bibles for God to love us, but we also knew that we would need spiritual strength for that new season in our lives. When we neglected the spiritual disciplines—such as prayer, Sabbath, community, and Scripture reading—we got out of shape, undernourished, and weak.

Often, when any of us takes on a new job or task, our responsibilities seem to work against what we need most during that time: a strong relationship with God. If you're feeling that way, prayerfully ask the following three questions.

1. Should I do different hard things?
Remember what we talked about in the second chapter—how God doesn't give conflicting obligations? If the hard thing you're

doing consistently conflicts with your relationship with God, it
could be that you're doing the right thing for the right reason at
the wrong time! And as our dad always says, "The right thing at
the wrong time is the wrong thing."

Grace had certain hard things in mind in her early twenties,
such as graduating from college, but she found that her planned
activities didn't seem in line with God's call.

> Just after I turned twenty-one, my dad's health failed, mak-
> ing him quite disabled. I saw my mother become so busy
> in the midst of all her worries that I wondered how she
> found the strength. I realized that the responsibilities I was
> used to were no longer enough for my family's needs. It
> also occurred to me that to withhold my help because I
> was busy with college was to withhold the love of God for
> my mother and father. I had to rearrange my thinking.
>
> Sometimes doing hard things now is as simple as smil-
> ing and giving my mother or father a hug even though
> I'm depressed that day. Other times, it means being willing
> to stay up late to finish a class assignment so I can clean
> the kitchen in the afternoon. If I love and care about what
> God wants of me, I must even be willing to take an extra
> semester to finish college.
>
> It's a battle of heart attitude, for if my heart isn't in the
> right place before God, my actions are worthless. It's a bat-
> tle to submit my ways to the Lord and follow His plans for
> my life, especially when they don't make sense.
>
> —Grace, age 22
> Berwyn Heights, Maryland

Grace found that she could not do all the hard things in front of her and still have an attitude that pleased God. Sometimes doing hard things means saying no to an exciting project in order to be faithful to your studies, to prioritize your relationship with God, or to be there for your family during a difficult time. You're not saying no to doing hard things; you're saying yes to *different* hard things.

2. Should I do more hard things?

If doing hard things is distracting you from God, it could be due to a lack of personal discipline. If you've allowed other things to crowd out your time with God, the solution may be to do *more* hard things and change the way you're using time to make time for your relationship with God.

Many people find that the morning is the best time to read the Bible and pray. Making time for God before the day starts can be a good launching pad for the rest of your day.

The morning, however, might not be the best time for you. Maybe the afternoon or just before bed is the time you're most alert and able to focus on God. What matters is that you make your time with God a top priority.

If you have free time in the day, how do you use it? Does it trickle away through video games, time online, or texting your friends? Or are you intentional about using that time to grow closer to God?

When we really think something is important, we'll make sure to give it our time as soon as we have a free moment—and we'll carve out those free moments if they don't come naturally. That's how it should be with our personal time with God.

3. Should I do fewer hard things?

Another case in which doing hard things can distract you from your relationship with God is when you're trying to do too much by yourself. When you're working on a big project, you need to remember the definition of "big hard things"—things that are *too big to be accomplished alone.*

For example, if all your free time is being taken up with phone calls, errands, and e-mails relating to your project (and you've already determined that simply being more disciplined with your time won't solve the problem), then find someone else who can take one or more of those things off your hands on a regular basis. It could be a sibling, friend, or parent. If you explain to others why what you're asking them to do is important and why you're asking them to take it off your hands, they will probably be glad to help. (We talked more about the benefits and challenges of working with a team in chapter 3.)

You might even find that the project goes more smoothly when each task gets the individual attention it deserves—or when someone who is naturally gifted in a certain area takes ownership of that job. Plus, good time with God each day will help you work together as a team with more love, patience, and understanding.

Keep in mind that the choice is never between doing hard things and our relationship with God, because God is the One who commands us to do hard things! Instead, we serve and obey God *by* doing hard things—with Christ as the center, His glory our goal, and holding every hard thing we do with open hands.

WHEN THE DOING GETS TOUGH

Keeping on in the middle of hard things

At our first conference in Sacramento in 2005, we booked a small facility and had to turn several hundred people away. It was a good problem to have, but very painful. This past year, we accidentally printed the wrong name for a church where one conference was held—on fifteen thousand brochures!

All of our conferences have problems, in fact—and they're always *different* problems. We've found that most of the hard things we do take longer than we think they will and that big journeys involve a lot of small steps, each with its own challenges.

When you anticipate this reality, you'll be better prepared to keep going when you feel stuck. You'll realize that difficult circumstances don't necessarily mean your hard thing was never meant to be. They are a part of the process—and a beautiful way for God to remind us how much we need Him.

Are you wondering, *What am I doing wrong? Why on earth did God choose me to lead this?*

If you're feeling ill equipped to do what you're doing, we have good news for you: God knew that from the beginning. And He is still able to complete His plans.

I want to see this through, but I feel overwhelmed. How do I keep up my enthusiasm?

One rebelutionary tells us, "My biggest disappointment or obstacle was that doing hard things isn't easy. Go figure. I'm still caught up in the idea of having things fast and easy, but becoming on fire for Christ is no fast and easy task, and I think that's the most humbling thing I've found."

Somewhere in the middle of doing hard things, almost everyone asks, *Is this worth it?*

At those points, we often need to examine our hearts for the sin of impatience. It sounds silly when you think about it, but our tendency can be to get impatient with God—as if He doesn't know best, is too slow, or isn't paying attention.

When our motivation for doing hard things is to grow, to obey God, and to glorify Him, we can persevere when faced with obstacles, delay, and even failure. When our response is to get impatient, that's a sign that *our* expectations rather than God's have crept in.

Impatience shows that although we want the benefits of doing hard things, we are not willing to pay the price—just like someone who wants to be in good shape but is not willing to push through a hard workout.

Whenever either of the two of us is tempted to doubt God or give up on something He has called us to do, we ask ourselves,

Did you really think there wouldn't be a cost? It is just another way of saying, *Did you really think doing hard things would be easy?*

Overcoming discouragement requires that we continually remind ourselves that growth is worth the pain. Hebrews 12:11 tells us, "For the moment all discipline seems painful rather than pleasant, but later it yields the peaceful fruit of righteousness to those who have been trained by it."

Zack's story is a powerful example of how God works even through circumstances beyond our control to shape us into who He wants us to be.

> When I was six years old, I was diagnosed with a stomach illness called Crohn's disease. Crohn's makes ordinary things, like school, very difficult to accomplish. Some days, the only thing I can do is focus on getting well. I have had to learn to deal with the physical pain and stress from the Crohn's as well as chemical depression. There have been times when I wished God would take me Home.
>
> But I hold on to the two things I know will not change: my family's love for me and an almighty God who will never leave me. God has helped me realize that He has a purpose for every person He creates—even people who have Crohn's. God allows things that are hard into our lives to help us become strong.
>
> During my lowest point in high school, I didn't know what I could possibly do for God that would make a difference. I felt that I could never do anything right. The Lord showed me that I didn't have to have a plan. I just needed to follow Him.

As I have been growing in the Lord, I feel that God wants me to be a Christian example in the business world. I want to start a business that is based on God's Word here in my hometown. After all, whether you become a preacher, plumber, lawyer, chemist, or the guy in charge of all pork products, you only have one real job: to reach people for Jesus.

Crohn's has actually been a blessing to me. God has used this constant struggle to teach me how to focus and keep my priorities straight. It has also made me a more compassionate person.

My advice to anyone who doesn't think life is worth living: hang on. Life gets better. It won't be terrible all the time. There is so much you can continue to do no matter the pain you're in right now. Even with setbacks, you can move forward.

—Zack, age 19
Decatur, Alabama

It would be natural for Zack to become impatient with God if he focused on current circumstances. But whether what you're doing was something thrust on you (like in Zack's life) or a project you chose to organize, faith is a choice—a choice to trust not your circumstances, yourself, or your plans but God.

When we acknowledge our dependence on God as we do hard things, we're telling Him and the people around us that it's not about us. Persevering in hardship, dreaming big, and staying faithful to God no matter the cost is one way to show Christ to others.

After all, people hanging up on you, venues falling through, microphones not working, friends disagreeing, medical setbacks, fatigue, donors backing out, and even facing your own weaknesses are not obstacles to doing hard things—they *are* hard things.

The most remarkable line in Zack's letter is "Crohn's has actually been a blessing to me." Those are words born out of great struggle, questions, and waiting. They speak to the "results" God is giving Zack: compassion, faith, and the ability to encourage others. Those results have come at a cost, but they are worth it.

Whether your weariness feels like a blessing now or not, God is aware of it. He is able to use it to bring about growth that reaches far beyond any human plans. Following God, even though things don't necessarily go as you'd hoped, is why you are doing hard things in the first place.

What if I try to do something hard and it doesn't work out? Does that mean I didn't hear God right?

When you're pursuing a calling God has laid on your heart and then your plans fall through, you might feel like you heard God wrong. You might even be tempted to feel as if God is displeased with you. But don't allow disappointment to keep you from trusting God's bigger vision for your life.

I was taking an evangelism class when the subject came up of doing another intensive class with the same program. As soon as I heard that, I thought, *I need to lead that.* I prayed about it for a couple weeks and felt sure I was

supposed to do it. I told our group that I would head this
up. They were glad someone would. All was going well.

I then started getting volunteers to help me. I sent out
e-mails asking if anyone would be willing to share their
testimony, help set up, or help in any way. I got just two
replies. I was a little disappointed, but I picked a date to do
the class and put it on the calendar.

I continued to pray about volunteers and what I
should say and do. I got two more offers of help. I was
very excited, thinking that this would come together. I was
wrong. After I announced the event date, people came up
to me and told me they couldn't come. I didn't hear from
anyone who could come. I tried my youth group. No one.

I finally had to cancel the event because no one would
commit to coming. I felt confused—I was so sure that God
had wanted me to do this. Now I know that it wasn't the
right time. But I haven't given up. I am going to keep
doing hard things for the glory of God.

—Elizabeth, age 15
Lubbock, Texas

It's virtually impossible to start doing a hard thing without
having a vision of what it will look like. It's important, in fact, to
have specific goals and work toward them. But we need to
remember that God is sovereign over even our well-meaning
plans.

Elizabeth knew what she wanted her evangelism class to look
like, how many people she wanted to volunteer, and when she
wanted it to be. She found out that all those details weren't *God's*
plan for that class. God might indeed have been calling her to

organize this hard thing—but in order to fulfill her ultimate vision of glorifying Him, not her immediate vision of leading a class.

Elizabeth's experience strengthened her faith in God's timing and perhaps helped purify some of her motivations. The process of organizing the event may have given her good ideas for future hard things. And now God is using her story to encourage readers of this book. Other spiritual benefits might come so subtly that Elizabeth will never know how important this experience was.

Take a look at a time in the apostle Paul's life when he started to answer God's call one way and then changed direction because God led him somewhere else:

[Paul, Silas, and Timothy] went through the region of Phrygia and Galatia, having been forbidden by the Holy Spirit to speak the word in Asia. And when they had come up to Mysia, they attempted to go into Bithynia, but the Spirit of Jesus did not allow them. So, passing by Mysia, they went down to Troas. And a vision appeared to Paul in the night: a man of Macedonia was standing there, urging him and saying, "Come over to Macedonia and help us." And when Paul had seen the vision, immediately we sought to go on into Macedonia, concluding that God had called us to preach the gospel to them. (Acts 16:6–10)

This may seem like a boring passage with a bunch of funny names in it, but if you look closely, you can see that God is teaching us important things about how He leads us to do His will. Put yourself in the apostles' shoes, and see what you learn.

First, notice that they knew they were not supposed to go to Asia. That's a lot like us sometimes. We know what we are *not* supposed to do, but we aren't so sure about what we *are* supposed to be doing.

Second, you see the apostles setting out for Bithynia. We can guess they probably sat down, talked, and decided that Bithynia was the place God wanted them to be. Imagine how easy it would have been for them to get discouraged when the Holy Spirit stopped them on the way to do what they thought God wanted them to do.

Those of us who have experienced God's slamming a door in our faces when we thought we were doing His will can relate to the confusion they may have been tempted to feel. *What is God up to? What does He want me to do?*

The most beautiful part of this story is the next line: "So...they went down to Troas." Now, this might not seem all that significant if you don't take into account the context. God kept them out of Asia. They thought God wanted them in Bithynia, but He kept them out of there too.

From a human standpoint, they had every reason to say, "God, we have no idea what You want us to do, and frankly we no longer care. Until You are willing to tell us plainly, we are going to stay here and get comfortable." But instead, in a radical display of faith in God's leading, *they kept moving*—they went down to Troas. In Troas, God sent a vision to Paul calling them to Macedonia, and they were able to go immediately—the door was wide open.

It may seem confusing that God waited until the apostles got to Troas to call them to Macedonia. It would have made more sense for Him to let them know right after He closed the door to Bithynia. But instead we see that God wanted them to keep going even after *two* doors had been closed. As they persevered in faith, He opened the door of opportunity.

We've experienced this kind of unexpected change on a variety of levels. When we were sixteen, for instance, we felt that God was calling us into filmmaking. We had a vision for a big film project we wanted to work on—and we got started writing the script. We even traveled to Texas for the inaugural San Antonio Independent Christian Film Festival.

But then a medical crisis in our family canceled those plans. It was easy to feel discouraged and confused. What we didn't realize was that God was clearing our schedule so that we could start the Rebelution, intern at the Alabama Supreme Court, and plan our first conference that fall.

We returned to the film festival the next year (and the next), but this time as press—live-blogging on TheRebelution.com. With greater access to the people involved in the festival, we became friends with veteran filmmakers and other rebelutionaries. Today, our younger brother Isaac is an aspiring filmmaker, working with many of the same young filmmakers we got to know as live-bloggers when we were his age.

What we once saw as disappointment, we now understand as God's good, wise, and sovereign guidance. His plan was far better than anything we could have imagined.

So if it seems like the hard thing you're pursuing just isn't meant to be, it could be that God has something even better for you. The result you had in mind—a finished project—might be different from the result God has in mind. He has important lessons to teach you through developing an idea or working with others or dealing with disappointment.

It could be that God is calling you to persevere in the same hard thing but to revise your original goal. If you believe something is right, never give it up lightly—unless it's conflicting with a clear command in Scripture. Godly mentors are primary resources to help you determine whether a closed door is a "No," a "Not yet," or a "Not this way."

Just because a giant obstacle stands in your path, that doesn't mean the door has closed. Just because your plans fell through doesn't mean your hard thing has failed. Either of these circumstances could mean that God wants to grow your faith by giving you the strength to overcome—or simply to see Him at work in a different way than you expected.

I'm doing hard things, but nothing feels different. What should I do?

So you read the book. You change your attitude. And you do hard things. Not just one hard thing, but three. A dozen. Small, big, medium. And nothing feels different. *Okay,* you wonder, *does this count? Shouldn't I be a different person by now?*

Reid's story offers an example of how God is working even when we do not see the immediate results we expected:

I have always been fearful getting up in front of people, and it seemed God was prompting me to take a speech class. The night before class sign-up began, I was arguing with God about the class. Reluctantly, I signed up, hoping it would be full.

But I got in.

The first speech came around, and I volunteered to go first. I felt like I was walking off a cliff because God told me to, and I just hoped His hand would hold me up. He delivered me then and in every speech after that as well.

I learned through this experience that God comes alive to us through hardships. I drew much closer to God and learned a lot about Him when I was faced with a great difficulty. I had to cling to Him and His promises.

I also learned that God does not take away your fear and then you do what He says. You do it, and if He desires, He will take away the fear.

Fear kept me relying on God during my class, and it still does. In fact, I am as fearful of speaking now as I was then. But I know that letting fear thwart God's plans for me is wrong. God taught me to trust Him more and more and to do what He says, letting Him take care of the outcome.

—Reid, age 20

Novi, Michigan

We might hope or even expect that our fear, doubt, insecurity, anger, or immaturity will go away when we do hard things. And they will—but on God's timetable, not ours.

In the meantime, God might have something better in mind, such as increasing our faith. After all, "faith is being sure of what we hope for and certain of what we do not see" (Hebrews 11:1, NIV). It is painful when we don't see the change we are looking for in ourselves and others. But if we are following God as humbly and intentionally as we know how, we can have faith that change is happening.

Reid found that God had a bigger plan than his ideas of how he would feel after taking speech class. His fearful feelings didn't change, but he trusted that his *act* of faith would change him. Even if God never takes away his fear of public speaking, Reid has learned that God can work in and through him despite his fears.

As we grow closer to God, we do experience new joy, maturity, and discipline. But if we rely on our own feelings to determine whether doing hard things is worth it, we're missing the point. The point of doing hard things is to glorify God. Feelings of satisfaction, spiritual growth, and excitement are the wonderful by-products God often gives us—in His time—when we follow Him.

If you've been doing hard things for a while and are disappointed with the results in *you,* consider what expectations you had. Expecting results in a few days or weeks would be like a farmer expecting to harvest his crops two weeks after planting them. Our attempts to do hard things place good seed in the ground. Then we wait for those seeds to bear a harvest.

God can and does grant seasons of rapid growth, but most of the time we cannot see growth from one day to the next. Looking back six months or a year is a better way to measure His work in our lives.

You might also talk with a parent or godly mentor about the changes he or she sees in you. Often others can encourage you to press on because they see changes you don't. Others can also help you determine whether you need to change something in your attitude or approach to hard things.

When you're doing hard things, you have a more objective gauge of your "success" than roller-coaster emotions or expectations. What is that gauge? It's God's truth. And the truth is that God is in you to finish the good work He began.

THE GUTS FACTOR

How to move against the crowd — and why

Changing the culture can be more fun in theory than it is in practice. It reminds us of writing a book. Growing up, we both thought it would be cool to write a book. We imagined telling people that we were authors, doing interviews, or even finding out that someone famous had read (and liked) what we wrote.

It didn't take very long after we started writing *Do Hard Things* to realize that what we really wanted was to *have written* a book. The actual writing wasn't exciting, fun, or rewarding. It was the hardest thing we've ever done—and the most stressful.

A lot of people want to be authors. Few people want to write a book. Changing the culture is like that. We want to be world changers, but we all have days when we don't want to do what it takes to change things. We wonder, *Will going against the flow be worth it? Does it mean saying goodbye to fun?*

Our quick answers are yes and no. Does that help clarify things? Well, don't worry. This chapter tackles those questions and more.

Am I missing out on anything because I'm not doing the "normal" things teens do?

Stephen, Melanie, and Dianna Muldrow did not have an "ordinary" summer this year. Instead of doing the relaxing things most people would expect three teenagers to do on vacation, these siblings wanted to make a difference in their city, Houston.

They decided to raise awareness—and money—for a cause they care deeply about: human trafficking. And they decided to do it in a big way, by organizing a concert featuring world-class musicians at Jones Hall, the home of the Houston Symphony.

"This was something that we started completely from scratch," Stephen tells us. "We haven't ever done anything like this, and our first contact with Jones Hall was a phone call asking what we needed to do to rent it. We wanted to reach as many people as possible, so we decided that the best way would be to have a concert and have someone talk about human trafficking during it."[1]

Human trafficking is a $32 billion industry that keeps 27 million people worldwide in slavery—working in sexual slavery, sweatshop factories, tourist industries, and other types of business. The United States Justice Department ranks Houston's I-10 corridor as one of the main routes of human trafficking in the nation.[2]

"When we first talked to some of our friends about human trafficking, they asked what it was," Melanie says. "When we told them what it was, they asked, 'So you mean in other countries?' No one expects it here in Houston.... I want to help the kids and families that are in trouble right now."[3]

The siblings met with politicians, business owners, and journalists. They rented the location, contacted musicians, and developed a website. As they were preparing for the concert, they spoke to more than fifteen hundred people in small-group settings about human trafficking and did numerous interviews with media.

At the end of August, the concert, which they named Broken Cords, drew six hundred people to Jones Hall to hear internationally touring musicians. The concert raised more than eleven thousand dollars for organizations fighting human trafficking in the Houston area.

You could argue that the Muldrows missed out on a typical teen summer—going to the mall, watching movies, and maybe working a part-time job. But as Stephen says, "We wanted to do something meaningful, something that had purpose to it."[4]

We love the creativity of the Muldrows's idea. We also love how it shows how "normal" and satisfying it can be to go beyond society's expectations.

If there is anything people have objected to about the Rebelution, it's that we're encouraging teens to grow up too fast. As if by choosing to do hard things they'll skip some critical "fun only" stage that is necessary for their development.

Does doing hard things mean growing up prematurely? If you view responsibility as a bad thing, a burden you have to carry around, then yes. If that's the case, putting off responsibility as long as possible is great.

But if you view responsibility as what it is—a muscle to be strengthened—then being responsible now is not premature at all. Just like working out at the gym, you don't go straight to the heaviest weights you can find. Instead, you start with what is hard for you right now and work your way up from there.

Some teens we've talked to think "growing up" means losing their sense of humor, not being able to have fun, and being stressed out all the time. It's true that adulthood brings a lot more responsibility, but one reason many adults exhibit the tendencies these teens have identified is because they're overwhelmed when that responsibility comes. They haven't worked up to it.

If we fail to prepare adequately as young adults, responsibility will be like a weight that is too heavy for our untrained arms. The problem will not be that we grew up too fast but that we weren't prepared when we did grow up and become adults. Rather than learn to properly balance hard work and fun as teenagers, we let a preoccupation with fun set us up for failure.

But if we assume that the teen years are about preparation, as they have historically and biblically been defined, we will become mature, competent, and responsible men and women who know when and how to have fun. With this understanding, "growing up" doesn't spoil the teen years; it is the fulfillment of the teen years lived well.

The Muldrows are planning to do another concert next year and are looking into doing concerts in other cities. As Stephen tells us, "For a summer of doing hard things, I would say that it was well worth it."[5]

Can doing hard things be fun?

When we were seventeen and interning at the Supreme Court of Alabama, we were invited to speak to a local youth group. We'd never done anything like that before, but we were excited about sharing some of the ideas we'd been developing on the Rebelution blog—like The Myth of Adolescence and Do Hard Things.

The day finally came and things were especially busy at the court. We were so busy that we ended up hopping in the car and heading to the church still in court attire (translation: suits and ties).

When we got to the church and started sharing with our fellow teens that the idea of the "teen years" is a recently developed concept and that our culture is robbing them by telling them to "just have fun," we could tell something was wrong. We told jokes, we told stories, we asked questions—but when we switched to a Q-and-A time, it became apparent that our attire was sending a different message than we intended.

"Do you always dress this nice?" one guy asked.

"Do you ever do anything for, like, just for fun?" asked another.

As soon as we realized the impression we were making, we quickly explained that we don't always wear suits (T-shirts and jeans are our outfits of choice), we love sports (basketball especially—we're short but we try really hard), we love music, we watch movies, we style our hair, and we even play video games from time to time. In a lot of ways, we're very ordinary guys.

After clarifying some more (and ditching the ties), we explained that being a rebelutionary means putting fun in its proper place. We try to view fun as a break from the "hard things" that we spend most of our time doing. We relax, hang out, and have fun after we accomplish something significant. Having fun is important—a workaholic's "hard thing" might be to take a break and relax!—but it's not the most important thing.

Our culture tells us that we should have fun first and do hard things only when we have to. It sounds great in theory, but in reality we're being robbed. Robbed of contentment in the future, effectiveness for God, character and competence, and maybe even the spouse we've always dreamed of (because we weren't prepared for him or her).

We also saw an opportunity that night in Alabama to explain that we have a different way of looking at fun—and it doesn't mean we miss out on our best life.

Here's a good example of how hard things can be a fun part of being a teen:

Last year, I decided I wanted to give my birthday to God. Two months of planning later, thirty of my friends and I spent my birthday hanging out with three large recent refugee families from Africa. The refugees spoke no English, which threw us off, but it didn't matter. We had a great time playing soccer and football with them, giving and receiving makeovers with the girls, making bracelets for each other, and eating the potluck my friends had contributed to. I told my friends that I didn't want to receive any presents (which I admit was hard) but that I knew the refugees would love donations.

My biggest fear was that this would seem weird to my friends and that they wouldn't even have the desire to come. To my surprise, it was the exact opposite. One of my non-Christian friends told me that a lot of kids wanted to serve other people but there didn't seem to be any fun opportunities, especially ones you could do with a bunch of your friends. She was thankful that I was putting this together.

In a couple of months we will have another day of

serving new families. But I have to say my birthday was a very special day I will never forget.

—Cathleen, age 17
San Diego, California

Cathleen's hesitancy to miss out on an ordinary "fun" birthday could have robbed her of a far more satisfying and memorable celebration. But when she pursued her unusual idea, she discovered that her peers enjoyed it as much as she did. They discovered the pleasure of serving others. What's more, it sounds as if serving refugee families is becoming a new normal among her group of friends.

When we interviewed teens for *Do Hard Things,* we asked each of them the same question: "Do you feel like you've missed out by not spending more time having fun?" Every one of them had the same answer: "Who said that doing hard things isn't fun?"

It's true that the two of us do fewer "fun things" than the average young adult, but you couldn't say we have less fun. We might spend less time playing video games, going to parties, and just hanging out, but we also have a blast doing what we do.

Time and time again, we have had other teens confirm our own experience: the joy and the fulfillment that come from doing what God has called us to do are a hundred times better than a trip to the mall or a night at the movies could ever be.

How do I let my friends know I've changed?

Even if you've been involved in church for years and have a strong relationship with Christ, your life changes once you decide to do hard things. Letting your friends know that you're living for Christ, that you won't be doing things you used to do, or that you will be doing some new things they consider weird is one of the hardest things you can do, whether you're ten, eighteen, or forty-two.[6]

Zyatuba found that living out a new life begins with not giving up.

Upon becoming a Christian two years ago, I wished God would give me grace to share His Word with other young people in my country. I simply waited upon the Lord. Then I realized that waiting was not enough. I needed to work at it.

But the young people at church, including my friends, could not take what I had to say seriously because they knew me before I became God's follower. That is to say, they knew my past sinful life and could not believe I was not one of them anymore. What made it worse was the fact that I was now speaking against the things that I had enjoyed before I became a Christian.

Despite their not believing me, I did not give up. I prayed to God to plant good seed in me that would bear fruit and be a living testimony so my friends could see Him by the way I lived my life. I started speaking in our youth meetings, which we have every Saturday. Some of my friends started getting the idea that I am God's child.

I know that God will grant me grace to speak to many more young people on a one-to-one level as well as to

crowds. My hope is that many young people around the
world will focus on God and stop clinging to sin.
   —Zyatuba, age 20
   Lusaka, Zambia

How do we let our friends know we've changed? We tell
them. We show them. If we really are different, we will be willing
to say so and then show it by our actions. If we can't do that,
either we have not really changed, or we care more about what
other people think than about what God thinks.

As Jesus said, "Everyone who acknowledges me before men,
I also will acknowledge before my Father who is in heaven, but
whoever denies me before men, I also will deny before my Father
who is in heaven" (Matthew 10:32–33). These are serious words.
Our acknowledgment of Christ isn't what saves us, but it does
show whether we are saved.

Besides our own integrity before Christ, if we care about our
friends, we will *want* to let them know what God is doing in our
lives and invite them to join us. This often means telling them
the things that first excited us, sharing what we first read, or
inviting them to join us in an activity or event (we talked more
about this in chapter 3).

If they aren't interested, or are even antagonistic, you
might lose some friendships. But don't let fear keep you from
standing up and speaking out. You'll be surprised by who will
respond to a "do hard things" challenge. Low expectations
might be shackling them. All they need is to see someone like
them who has broken free, and they'll realize that their chains
are illusory.

Remember, even if your current friends respond negatively, you don't know who else might be watching and the impact you will have on them—and the new friendships that could be born as a result. As Zyatuba did, we can pray and trust that our words and actions will bear good fruit, even if we can't see it just yet.

What if doing hard things makes me unpopular?

We've received a lot of criticism, both directly and behind our backs, since we started the Rebelution. Some people believe we are encouraging young people to grow up too fast. Others have picked apart our writing or speaking styles. Sometimes the criticism seems unfair, and that's hard. Other times we know it's true, and that's even harder.

When people bring criticism to us directly, our prayer is always to learn from it, regardless of the attitude with which it's given. We've also learned that criticism comes with the territory. Our goal is not to make everyone happy but to do what we believe is right and pleasing to God.

It's probably true that a person who makes it through life without making any enemies never stood up for anything important. If you are doing something important for the kingdom of God, certain people will avoid you or even persecute you.

Persecution in your life might look like snubbing, teasing, rumor spreading, or even losing a friendship. When that kind of thing happens, it's usually because you are being effective—whether you are openly talking about God or simply standing up for what you believe in, as Erika did.

Recently, all the seniors in my high-school government class had to do a political action project. Most of the kids in my class were doing issues that were fairly minor. One group's issue was to put another skate park in our county. Another group's issue was to legalize marijuana. (This gives you a picture of what my school is like.)

I felt that God wanted me to do something bigger than what everyone else was doing: take a pro-life stance on the issue of abortion, a stance that is extremely unpopular in my school.

My best friend, Joanna, and I found two other girls passionate about this topic and began working on the project. Soon after we started, we had a minor communication problem that blew up into an ugly monster, resulting in two group members leaving to do their project on pro-choice rights—totally changing their stance on abortion.

Then my teacher, who is pro-choice, said we couldn't use any type of image in our presentation because we'd be using "shock value" to get our point across. After telling him we would have facts along with the pictures to educate our peers on the truth of abortion, he let us use first-trimester abortion pictures and medical diagrams of abortion.

The hardest part of the whole thing was when we got up and spoke to our peers about the injustice of abortion. Out of the twenty-five students we spoke to, two were pro-life. My stomach was in knots and I felt like I could pass out, but Joanna and I had done our research and presented it in a very open-minded manner.

Everyone listened intently to our presentation, especially the guys. I was shocked by how many questions we received and how many comments I heard, like, "That's messed up!" The day after the presentation, a friend who had watched the presentation and is not usually open to other viewpoints came over to me and said, "Your presentation was very powerful, Erika. I don't usually think that way, but you did a really good job presenting!"

This was the hardest thing I've done so far. I experienced so many sleepless nights, long work hours, broken friendships, and hurtful words regarding my stance that at times I didn't think I was going to be able to pull it off. But I kept saying to myself, *I'm doing hard things for Jesus! And with Him as my strength, I can do anything!*

—Erika, age 18

Watsonville, California

In his book *Crazy Love,* Francis Chan describes life as a never-ending downward escalator. In order to follow God, we have to sprint back up the escalator—and put up with all the perturbed glances and harsh words of those we bump into along the way. If we're not encountering any opposition, it's probably because we're just going with the crowd.

Our first response to persecution should be gratitude. That's right. We should rejoice! God has allowed us to join some pretty good company—including Jesus Himself, the apostles, and the prophets. If we are being persecuted because we are standing up for what is right and godly, we can consider ourselves blessed.

The night before He was betrayed, Jesus shared with his disciples: "If the world hates you, know that it has hated me before it hated you. *If you were of the world, the world would love you as its own; but because you are not of the world, but I chose you out of the world, therefore the world hates you.* Remember the word that I said to you: 'A servant is not greater than his master.' If they persecuted me, they will also persecute you" (John 15:18–20).[7]

An important thing to remember, though, is that Jesus and the apostles did not *seek* the disapproval of others. No one knew better than the apostle Paul what it was like to be persecuted, and yet he wrote, "If it is possible, *as far as it depends on you,* live at peace with everyone" (Romans 12:18, NIV). We live to draw others to God. God's thoughts toward us are more important than what others think, one way or the other.

If you are facing persecution in your family or at school, ask yourself, *Am I being persecuted because I am doing something for God or because I am being a difficult person to live with? Am I holding on to my cause so tightly that I can't see how it is hurting others, or are my actions showing others who God is? Am I more interested in what God thinks of me than in whether I am popular or unpopular?*

The two of us have to ask ourselves, *Is our first response to a negative e-mail defensiveness or humility?* If it's a criticism that comes up a lot, we have to ask, *Is there a more effective way we can communicate our message?* or, *Is there any truth to this observation that we need to address?*

Our goal as Christians is not to avoid getting into trouble. It's also not to *try* to get into trouble. Our goal is to get into the *right kind* of trouble. The right kind of trouble for Erika was doing her assignment as instructed, with her teacher's permission, and then speaking truth in front of her peers whether they were receptive or not.

If you believe you are doing what is right and pleasing to God, continue doing it. Easier said than done, huh? You might be surprised, though, at how your friends appreciate your sticking to your beliefs. Seeing your enthusiasm and commitment might change their opinion of you and what you believe, as Erika found. It might even motivate them to join you. If not, that's their decision—not yours.

How should rebelutionaries relate to pop culture—like TV, music, movies, books, and the Internet?

A lot of teens want to know, "If I'm a rebelutionary, does that mean I can't read/watch/listen to [insert pop culture reference]?" That question doesn't have a simple answer. Some of the stuff out there is good. Some of it, like pornography, is clearly wrong. But a lot of what is out there falls in between.

So how can we decide what to watch, read, and listen to?

In most cases, we can't give you a definite yes or no about a particular series of books or a blockbuster movie. But we do want to give you some tools for discerning whether something is influencing you for good or for bad. Christians have freedom in Christ—but it's that relationship with Christ that equips, motivates, and requires us to exercise discernment and seek to honor God in our entertainment choices.

One of the key principles of the Rebelution is what we call "the power of companionship." It's based on Proverbs 13:20: "Whoever walks with the wise becomes wise, but the companion of fools will suffer harm." This verse tells us that we become like our friends—for good or bad. If we want to be wise, mature, and godly, we need to spend time with people who are like that.

If we don't want to be foolish, immature, and worldly, we have to avoid spending time with people who are like that. In the New Testament, the apostle Paul gives an even stronger warning: "Do not be deceived: 'Bad company ruins good morals'" (1 Corinthians 15:33).

Studies show that the average American teen watches twenty-three hours of television every week and spends hours more online. What does that have to do with Proverbs and 1 Corinthians? Our companions are not limited to our family and friends. Our companions are the books, magazines, and graphic novels we read. Our companions are the movies, TV shows, and online videos we watch. Our companions are the video games we play, the websites we surf, the music we listen to, and even the clothes we wear.

Most of us don't think of these things as companions—and that is why media of any kind is such a powerful culture weapon. While we may be careful about our human companions, we give little thought to the countless nonhuman companions with whom we spend more time than most of our "real" friends.

If you stop and think about it, it's pretty ironic how much of what young people consider "cool" is controlled by middle-aged advertisers. And movies, TV shows, music, books, and magazines don't just address us at the level of social expectations; they dictate those expectations—and drive them lower.

Of course, the primary motivation for most television executives, record labels, movie producers, and publishing companies is not creating edifying, high-quality content for teens and tweens—it's to get your money. Corporate culture shapers have found that teens who buy in to low expectations are much more likely to buy their products. And that's why popular culture usually appeals to the very worst in teens: insecurity, envy, lust, greed, laziness, vanity, and the endless obsession with "cool."

This doesn't mean we have to avoid all pop culture products. But it does mean we need to be extra careful about how we use our time. Our lives are not our own. Rachel found that weeding ungodly influences out of her life had an even greater benefit than she had expected:

About two years ago, my family moved from the town I'd grown up in to a totally unfamiliar place. I was angry, insecure, and very alone. I fell into the trap of dressing and acting a certain way to try to feel good. I tried to find my security in looking "cool"—and only found unhappiness. Joy was not in my vocabulary.

Then one night when I was feeling especially distant from God and rejected by friends, God took hold of my heart while I was sitting alone in my bedroom. I began to cry—something I'd always hated doing because I didn't like being vulnerable. But that night I found that being vulnerable with my Savior was the only thing that could start the healing process in my life. I poured out all my hurt and anger, laying it all at my Savior's feet, and I felt God's love in an incredible way.

As I started searching for what it meant to truly follow Christ, the flaws in my life shocked me. For example, I had never dressed in a way that I thought was immodest, but I saw how insensitive I was being to my brothers in Christ through some of my styles. I went to my dad and did one of the hardest things I've ever done: I apologized for the way I had been dressing and asked him to go through my clothes with me and throw away everything he didn't like. I survived that night, but a lot of my wardrobe didn't. In the following days, I survived weeding through the movies I watched, the books I read, and the things I said.

My entire attitude changed, and it wasn't always easy. But let me tell you, I now know joy. I now have peace and security because of my identity in Christ. It's true that people don't always understand my convictions. But I have something from them I didn't have before: respect. People know I live my faith. I fail sometimes, but Christ is always there to pick me up and point me in the right direction. I may not be visibly "rewarded" when I dress, talk, and act differently than other teens, but my reward in Christ is beyond measure.

—Rachel, age 16
Winona Lake, Indiana

Sometimes it takes asking a wise adult, as Rachel asked her dad, to help us figure out how to engage with culture without submitting to it. For example, if you aren't sure whether a particular book would be helpful or harmful to read, ask a godly person you respect to check it out and tell you if they think reading it would be a good investment of time. If they say yes but offer caution, ask them if they would read it at the same time as you; then get together and talk about it as you go. Not only can talking through a book with someone else help you sort out truth from lies, but also it gives you accountability. If you find your relationship with God hurting, you will have support in turning away from it. The same thing is true for movies, music, clothes, or anything else.

You will not change culture by serving culture. As you make decisions about what to allow into your mind and heart, ask yourself, *Does this draw me closer to God or take me further away?* Your answer will either free you to enjoy something new or free you to let go of something that keeps you from what is most important.

NOW WHAT?

When doing is done

Whenever we finish a hard thing—whether it's a big school assignment, a speaking trip, or writing this book—we experience a wide range of thoughts and emotions. *We're done! Is it okay to be proud about this? What can we learn from this experience? Can we take a nap?* And of course, the biggest question: *Now what?*

If you're asking similar questions at the end of your own big project, here are some things to keep in mind as you prepare for your next adventure to begin.

Is it all right to feel proud after doing a hard thing?

In the moments or days after completing a particularly big project, it's natural to feel excited, satisfied, even relieved! In moments like that, it can be easy to start feeling proud as well. You feel good about yourself and what you accomplished. Is that okay?

When we look at God's Word, we see that, with the right attitude, the enthusiasm we feel after doing something hard points us right back to God. Consider the unrestrained joy of the psalmist in what God has done:

> We will shout for joy when you are victorious
>> and will lift up our banners in the name of our
>>> God....
> Some trust in chariots and some in horses,
>> but we trust in the name of the LORD our God....
> O LORD, the king rejoices in your strength.
>> How great is his joy in the victories you give!...
> Be exalted, O LORD, in your strength;
>> we will sing and praise your might.
>>> (Psalm 20:5, 7; 21:1, 13, NIV)

In many of the psalms and throughout Scripture, we can sense the excitement godly people have in seeing God answer prayer and help His people. This same excitement comes through in many of the letters the two of us receive about teens doing hard things and seeing God work through them to serve others.

In every moment of victory, God calls us to remember that we can do good things only when He works through us. Our response to accomplishing a hard thing will never be perfectly pure, but as we grow closer to God, our desire to see *Him* glorified, not us, will grow. Our excitement over what He has done will practically burst from us! We will take more and more joy in being part of what God is doing.

That's why godly excitement over doing a hard thing leads not to pride but to humility. We have the wonderful privilege of responding to God's call, joining Him in His work, and seeing our faithful obedience bear fruit.[1]

Has God allowed you to be a part of something He is doing in the world? Has He gifted you in certain ways and provided the resources, perseverance, and energy to accomplish something? Rejoice! You have a great opportunity to celebrate what God has done—and what He has allowed you to help Him accomplish.

How do I keep from falling back into my old ways of thinking and acting?

Anyone who has ever tackled a big project and brought it to completion knows there is a letdown afterward. It's like the tired contentedness you feel after a good workout. The danger is that when we are tired and let down our guard, we tend to go right back into old habits. That's because our old patterns are familiar and comfortable to us.

Many people slip into old patterns because they fail to understand a basic principle of life: *changing something in your life requires changing something in your life.* This might seem obvious—and redundant—but you would be surprised how many people (including us!) sometimes forget it entirely.

Another way of saying the same thing is, *If you always do what you've always done, you will always get what you've always gotten.* It's not enough to *feel* different; we have to *act* different. Our feelings will fluctuate, but our actions do not need to fluctuate with them. Here are some suggestions for making permanent change.

Cut Things Out

What triggers your retreat to your old life? Is it something you can cut off, such as a friendship, a subscription, or the television? Is it something you can throw out, such as books, movies, or clothes? Do it.

Why would you keep what tempts you to fall back into your old ways? Is it because you're not quite ready to give it all up yet? Then you need to be honest about that. But now—when you're excited about doing hard things and ready to see a difference—is the time to make drastic changes.

Jesus said, "If your right hand causes you to sin, cut it off and throw it away" (Matthew 5:30, NIV). In other words: it's not worth it. The cost of keeping what causes you to sin is too great.

Andrew's story captures this idea well. He writes that he recently rededicated his life to Christ and then began making a lot of practical changes.

Soon after I rededicated my life to Christ, I grabbed a garbage bag. I combed through everything in my room, every little thing. I looked through my shelves, asking God to show me what I needed to be free of. I threw about twenty books in the bag. Then came my music. It was hard to do, but I threw most of it in the bag too. I grabbed my phone and deleted some numbers of people who did not share in my lifestyle of following after Christ. I even took things I had written and ripped them up and threw them away if I knew they were not pleasing to God.

In the end, I was amazed at how heavy the bag was—at how many things in my life I had allowed to influence me that did not lead to Jesus. It was an awesome experience, and the relief I felt afterward was something only God could provide.

—Andrew, age 15
Mission, Texas

You might also be amazed at how heavy the garbage bag of your old life is! Although this tactic is actually one of the easiest ways to get rid of your former habits, not every temptation can be eliminated. But don't be discouraged. Though fighting temptation is a lifelong battle, once you throw out what you can, you will feel a freedom you couldn't have predicted beforehand.

Rearrange the Furniture

If something in your life triggers your old habits and you can't get rid of it completely, consider how you can make it less of a priority.

As an example, say you decided that you were going to stop watching TV and focus on reading that big stack of books you keep saying you'll get to someday. But all the furniture in your living room is arranged in a semicircle around the television, with the remote resting on the arm of your chair.

Guess what is going to happen?

One day you'll be sitting in your chair, reading Wayne Grudem's *Systematic Theology,* and you'll look up at the television and it will look back at you. And it will seem so lonely and blank. And then you'll remember that your favorite show is on.

And. You'll. Watch. TV.

Why? Not because you weren't really committed at the beginning, but because feelings aren't enough to carry you—or anyone—through these kinds of changes.

If you really wanted to follow through with your commitment, you would rearrange the furniture in the living room, put away the remote, and unplug the television—maybe even put it in the garage or on the curb. That kind of change is much more likely to succeed. You will have used your initial excitement to fuel changes in your life that make it harder for you to slip back into old patterns.

Kristin's story is a great example of using spiritual excitement to make a practical change:

> As I thought about what hard thing God was calling me to do, I felt that God wanted me to deal with my friends. The friends I had were not the best, especially the group of people I always ate lunch with. I decided to make a change. I moved to an empty table at lunchtime. I sat alone. And for the first time, I was scared about who would accept me. Finally, after lunch was half over, my friend Erica came and sat next to me. So we sat there until we could find a new table where we fit in. I've lost a lot of friends for not sitting at my old table. But I'd rather sacrifice friendship than sacrifice my relationship with God.
> —Kristin, age 18
> Coopersville, Michigan

Kristin didn't rely on her feelings alone to change her friendship habits. She made a concrete change—a change that would remind her of her former convictions even if her feelings changed.

Ask for Forgiveness

Let's be honest. Sometimes all it takes is an argument with a parent and we feel as if we're back where we started: impatient, angry, and confused. Our rebelutionary mind-set just doesn't seem strong enough for the dinner table. And family relationships are not something we can cut off!

This leads us to the reality of living the Christian life. *Growing* as a Christian means just that—growing. We don't arrive right away. We are in process, and that fact alone can be very humbling, as Justin discovered:

> Since the beginning of high school, I've worked at a local Christian bookstore. All the employees at the bookstore receive thirty free books every quarter and a discount on other books. To put it lightly, I have a lot of books.
>
> But I became greedy. I started returning books for store credit and then getting other books I wanted that had just come in. It was a form of theft.
>
> I convinced myself that what I had done was not sin. I argued with God. I finally said, "Fine! I'll make this right."
>
> I walked into the store practically shaking. When I learned the manager was at a meeting, I was relieved. I did, however, write out a confession naming sins I had committed against the company. I put my letter on top of his desk and left.
>
> Soon my manager called. I was nervous, not knowing what to expect. The first words out of his mouth were, "Justin, you are forgiven. That took a lot of guts." Can I scream freedom and joy!

Now I know that sin doesn't have dominion over me.
Joy comes from being free from sin! This was a hard thing
worth doing.
　　—Justin, age 20
　　Zeeland, Michigan

As rebelutionaries, we respond to failure differently than we
used to. We recognize that we are people in need of grace. We ask
for forgiveness—from God and from the people we hurt. Having
to ask for forgiveness for the same thing again and again might
be the best motivation to live our new lives!

Be Realistic

Sometimes young people who attend our conferences or read our
first book get very excited, and that excitement translates into,
My life is going to completely change right now and forever. With such
extreme expectations, when something or someone inevitably
squashes their enthusiasm, they revert to their old lives. They
recover and get back on track, but these experiences discourage
them.

"What did I do wrong?" one young man asked us. "I was on
such a spiritual high when I left your conference, but all it took
to bring me crashing down was getting into an argument with
my younger brother."

Jesus told a story about what this looks like in the spiritual
life:

A farmer went out to sow his seed. As he was scattering the
seed, some fell along the path, and the birds came and ate
it up. Some fell on rocky places, where it did not have

much soil. It sprang up quickly, because the soil was shal-
low. But when the sun came up, the plants were scorched,
and they withered because they had no root. Other seed
fell among thorns, which grew up and choked the plants.
Still other seed fell on good soil, where it produced a
crop—a hundred, sixty or thirty times what was sown.
(Matthew 13:3–8, NIV)

Your rebelutionary mind-set might have sprung up quickly.
There's nothing wrong with that! It's natural to be excited about
changes you are making in your life, especially if you are making
those changes along with a group of other young people. But you
need to be planted in good soil—soil that is dependent on God,
not on circumstances, for sun and water.

We call this the Life Is Not a Coca-Cola Commercial principle. When we're feeling motivated and excited, it can seem as if
the whole world is nothing but smiling people, cheerful animals,
and sunny days. Then we get back into our regular routine,
receive bad news, or really blow it, and our happy delusion that
everything was going to be easy evaporates. Our motivation often
goes with it. Before we know it, we're back where we started with
seemingly no progress made.

If you base your life as a rebelutionary on not failing, you will
not be a rebelutionary for long. Assuming you can live without
making mistakes is just another form of pride.

It's a good thing your qualifications for the role are not based
on what *you* do but on what *God* does. You are not dependent on
whether you feel excited, motivated, or capable. You are not
dependent on living perfectly. You are dependent on God. And
that is rich soil to grow in.

Tell Somebody

One great way to break old habits is to enlist the help of a godly friend or mentor. Tell that person the specific habits you are trying to break. Tell him or her what is most likely to lead you into that habit.

This can be a humbling experience, but humility is a trademark of a rebelutionary. Allowing someone else to hold you accountable can be a very effective means of breaking old habits.

Strengthen Your Relationship with God

In Philippians, Paul reminds us that God's peace guards our hearts and our minds. To know that peace, he urges, "Whatever is true, whatever is noble, whatever is right, whatever is pure, whatever is lovely, whatever is admirable—if anything is excellent or praiseworthy—think about such things. Whatever you have learned or received or heard from me, or seen in me—put it into practice. And the God of peace will be with you" (4:8–9, NIV).

The more we are immersed in the things of God—the images, sounds, relationships, ideas, thoughts, and actions that please Him—the more real He becomes to us. The more we love what God loves, the more aware we are when we are slipping into our former ways of thinking and acting. Old habits lose their appeal. We want to leave those choices behind because they are such a contrast to the God we are getting to know more.

What should I do when I'm done with a hard thing? Is it okay to take a break?

Like many fifteen-year-old guys, Austin Gutwein loves basketball. Unlike most fifteen-year-old guys, however, Austin has used his love for hoops to raise over a million dollars for children and their families in Africa.

Hoops of Hope started in 2004, when Austin was nine years old. That spring he saw a video by the Christian humanitarian organization World Vision about children who had lost their parents to HIV/AIDS. As he thought about how devastated he would be to lose his parents, Austin decided he had to act.

After begging his dad to let him do something, Austin got in touch with World Vision. The next thing he knew, they were having a conference call. And after taking stock of his talents and interests, they came up with a simple idea: free throws.

"We decided that I would shoot free throws in honor of the kids who were orphaned due to HIV/AIDS," Austin explains.[2] To be exact, 2,057 free throws—one for each child who would be orphaned that school day by HIV/AIDS.

On December 1, 2004—World AIDS Day—ten-year-old Austin shot his 2,057 free throws. Individuals in his community had agreed to sponsor him, raising more than three thousand dollars for World Vision, enough to help eight orphans. But Austin wasn't satisfied.

"The second year I went up to my dad and told him, 'Hey, Dad, I want to shoot free throws again, but this time I want to get one thousand of my friends to join me,'" Austin says, laughing. "He kind of gave me that look."[3]

That year Austin and his dad went around to dozens of churches and schools and told them about Hoops of Hope. Austin reached his goal—one thousand friends shooting free throws for orphans—and raised thirty-five thousand dollars. And even then he wasn't satisfied.

In the four years since, Austin's organization has raised

enough funds to build a school, three medical centers, a water system, and two orphanages as well as provide thousands of medical kits and hundreds of bicycles and mosquito nets for caregivers in Zambia.[4] Each year the goal gets bigger, and every year thousands of young people around the world shoot free throws to bring hope and help to orphans they'll probably never meet.

Austin has been featured nationally on major television networks. He has traveled more than ten thousand miles to Twachiyanda, Zambia, for the opening of the school he helped to build, arriving as the guest of honor. He recently published a book called *Take Your Best Shot: Do Something Bigger than Yourself.*

But all those things don't make Austin a rebelutionary. What makes Austin a rebelutionary is the consistency of his attitude through the starts and stops of his projects. Austin took one simple idea—a relatively "small" hard thing—and it led to another. And another. As his abilities, age, and resources grew, he was able to do more. But his desire to do hard things for God's glory in God's time stayed the same.

That perspective is important to keep in mind when you've done one hard thing and are wondering what to do next— whether you've raised thousands of dollars for a good cause or finished your final exams.

Sometimes after a conference, for instance, all we can think is, *Whew, it's over!* If it's been a particularly grueling tour, we feel like crashing on the couch and not getting up for a week. The last thing we want to think about is tackling another big project.

And we do try to establish a rhythm for the hard things we do. We've found that if we never take a break, we burn out. On a day-to-day level, we need to know how to put our work aside in order to get enough sleep and not neglect our families. On a week-to-week level, God has given us a Sabbath rest—a day once a week, whether on Sunday or another day—to put aside our work and acknowledge our dependence on Him.

In the same way, when you finish a big project, it is appropriate to take some time to recuperate. We can't give you a formula for how much "break" time to take because it depends on how much time, money, and energy your last project demanded of you and your team. It also depends on your personality, whether time alone or time with people tends to feed you spiritually, and what else is going on in your life.

The most important thing is not how much time you take between projects but whether you are alert during that time to what God is calling you to do next. And one of the great things about doing hard things is that even if you need to rest a bit afterward, God uses one hard thing to motivate you to do another.

Austin discovered this in shooting hoops. Jed discovered it before church one Sunday.

A teenage guy who went to my church sat fairly close to my family every Sunday, but he didn't seem to enjoy coming, and no one ever talked to him.

I knew that I would have about ten minutes to talk to him before church started, but I was hesitant. I knew his name, but did he know mine? What if I introduced myself to him as if we had never met—would he be offended because he had been there the whole time? What if he didn't say anything at all when I talked to him?

But God reminded me of the mercy He had shown me and gave me courage to talk to this guy. So I did.

Overall, things went fine. He responded agreeably, and we had a fine conversation. Since then, I have continued to talk with this guy fairly regularly. Although I have not yet shared the gospel with him, I have recently started to consider more how I can take this next step.

And what grace God lavished on me! After I did this hard thing, God filled me with a greater desire to reach out and talk to those who have few friends in my church.

—Jed, age 18

Fairfax, Virginia

"After I did this hard thing, God filled me with a greater desire..." The thing is, you never *really* take a break from doing hard things. Once you are a rebelutionary, your mind-set changes, just as Austin's and Jed's did. You may not always be organizing some gigantic project, but you are always *looking* for ways to serve God and others in small, everyday ways.

It is also important to remember that rest itself can be active. You're not taking a break; you're getting ready for the next hard thing, drawing closer to God, and growing in other areas. Active resting and waiting means spending more time in prayer and Bible reading, more time with family and friends, more time spent alone thinking and planning, and more time spent reading great books that challenge your mind.

God has promised to use you for His kingdom if you are open to His leading. He has promised to do hard things through you because they were His idea in the first place. He has promised to finish the work already begun in you. Whether you are at the beginning, in the middle, or at the end of doing a particular hard thing, you can be sure that God is preparing you for something more.

PUTTING IT ALL TOGETHER

Two stories that will answer all your questions (or at least give you some great ideas)

Over the last few years, we've gotten to know hundreds of rebelutionaries around the world. We couldn't think of a better way to end this book than to let you in on the stories of two of them: Ana Zimmerman and John Moore. Their stories encompass many of the questions in the book and help bring many of these ideas together.

No longer silent: Ana's story

"We just plunged into the deep end," fifteen-year-old Ana says now about her work to host a Love the Least event in her hometown of Ithaca, New York. "It was God, because if we had known just *how* hard it would be, we might have hesitated."

Starting Small

Ana Zimmerman's big idea grew out of something much smaller: a research paper for school.

"I was working on a paper about abortion in ninth grade," she tells us. "I came across the website of an organization called Abort73. I had always considered myself pro-life, but I was shocked at what I saw. I could no longer be silent."[1]

Ana bought some Abort73 shirts and started trying to educate people around her about abortion. Shortly afterward, she read *Do Hard Things*. Inspired, she led a group study of the book—then started looking for something they could do together.

"I knew the message of the book wouldn't change anyone's life unless we put it into action," she explains. "I wanted to find something we could do together that would challenge all of us to do hard things."

When Ana read about partnering with Abort73 to host a Love the Least event in her local area, she knew she had found her project. The purpose of the event was exactly what she already knew God wanted her to do—to educate high-school and college students about abortion and equip them to make a difference.

It didn't take Ana and her family long to talk and pray about the idea. They all knew it was the right thing to do. Soon the planning began.

Gathering a Team

One of Ana's first steps was to organize her team. Her younger sister, Melody, became her closest ally for the event. Her parents

served as advisors and jacks-of-all-trades. Even her eight-year-old
brother, Jason, got involved—patiently tagging along and comforting his sisters when stress got the better of their emotions.

But as Ana started to recruit more members of her *Do Hard
Things* study group, she was surprised at how difficult it was. She
delegated jobs like fund-raising, publicity, printing flyers, and
prayer to friends who'd agreed to help—and expected things to
move quickly. It didn't take long for her to realize that wasn't
going to happen.

"After a few weeks, I realized my friends were waiting for *me*
to tell them exactly what to do," she tells us. "We went through
several people on some jobs before someone finally stuck with it."

Ana wrestled with how much to push people to do what they
said they would do. "That was tough," she says. "It's so easy for
me to take over and just do it. That was probably the hardest
thing for me. I'd see things that weren't getting done, and I'd
want to freak out. But I realized that I needed to help others rise
up and do hard things too. There comes a point where you just
have to let go and trust others. You can't control it."

Ka-Ching, Ka-Ching

Ana ended up with a core team of four people, plus her family.
Her friend Jamie was responsible for organizing weekly prayer
meetings and working with an older, more experienced prayer
leader. Another friend, Carrie, was in charge of coordinating
fund-raising to cover the costs of equipment rental, transportation, and publicity. Ana also wanted to raise enough money to
give Abort73 an additional offering at the event. "I never told
Ana, but I felt really discouraged when she told me we had to

raise four thousand dollars," Carrie admits. "I never thought we'd be able to reach that goal."

The team started organizing fund-raisers about a month after they took on the project, seven months before the event. They did a can and bottle drive, planned a Valentine's Day sale, and put on a pancake breakfast. Ana wrote a short article for their local crisis pregnancy center's newsletter to raise awareness about the event.

When we asked Ana for advice about approaching people to give money, host a fund-raiser, or publicize an event, she said, "Just do it. Don't think about it a lot before you make the phone call. Just grab the phone and dial the number. There's no easy way out. Once you get the hang of what you're supposed to say—'Hi, I'm the local coordinator for Love the Least'—it gets easier. Your comfort zone grows."

Getting the Word Out

Ana and her team made a list of thirty churches and twenty-five college campus groups to contact and ended up making presentations to twenty-three of them.

In each presentation, the team showed the Love the Least promo video from Abort73 ("By the fifth or sixth one, we could recite the whole thing backward and forward," Ana recalls, laughing) and shared a little bit about *Do Hard Things*. They also made out forms so people could respond with ways they could help—sending out e-mails, posting flyers, donating money, or joining the prayer team.

There were surprises along the way. One youth group of middle schoolers did not know what abortion was. "I was almost in tears as I told them—I didn't know how to explain it," Ana says. "But they were so open. It was amazing. And the pastor said that they would go and present to other churches. When we'd first walked in, we thought, *What are these little kids going to do?* But God sure proved us wrong."

Ana's team used a local community center for their fund-raisers. They advertised ahead of time in the local newspaper and on a local Christian calendar e-mail list. They charged a flat fee for each meal and had a donation bucket.

Trying to get churches involved was discouraging at times. They only got a few of their response cards back. One pastor told them, "We don't want anything to do with that!" Several of the college groups they talked to were skeptical about teenagers asking them to do something—and barely responded at all. Often when Ana passed around their e-mail sign-up sheet, people just kept passing it without even looking at it.

We mention these discouragements because sometimes in the excitement of a big hard thing, it can be easy to forget all the small things—and many disappointments—that go into a successful project. It's all part of the process of doing hard things.

One creative way Ana and her team raised money was to present the event to churches and then ask those churches to have a Love the Least Funding Sunday. They raised thousands of dollars through churches that took a special offering for the event.

As Ana's friend Jamie told us, no matter what happens when you present an idea to a pastor, church, or group, you have "to trust in the Lord that those seeds are planted and that He'll do what He wants to do with them."

In the Middle of a Battle

Fighting for the unborn went against the cultural norm in Ithaca, a town that (in Ana's words) "is open to almost anything except Christianity."

In order to publicize the Love the Least event, Ana wrote a letter to the editor of the local paper drawing parallels between the Jewish Holocaust and abortion. She included an invitation to the event at the end. Some people responded with rage, calling her a bigot and "all sorts of names." Posters Ana put up at her high school got torn down. When her dad put one up on his workplace bulletin board, it was taken down and stapled up again—backward.

This kind of persecution—along with hundreds of e-mails, phone calls, and details about the event itself—started to wear Ana and her team down. "Sometimes I would wonder, *Am I the right person to do this?*" Ana tells us. "But my dad reminded me to pray and see what God was trying to teach me through this. It helped to get my focus on the Lord and off myself."

"If I just looked at myself and my abilities, it was easy to get discouraged," she explains. "I had never done something like this before. But God was teaching me to rely on Him. I could not make this happen. I could not change people's hearts. I had to trust that God would pull this together."

I Think God Can, I Think God Can...

Ana and her team saw the power of low expectations firsthand. "It's a lot harder to do something when you're not expected to do it," Ana's sister told us.

Preparing for one of many presentations at a church, Melody was told to make sure she brought an adult along—since she was "just a middle schooler." Melody felt crushed, but she did the presentation anyway. "If she hadn't said that, I would have been able to do the same thing," she says. "Her response just made it seem harder."

Other adults at churches Ana and her team contacted simply didn't want to have anything to do with such a hot topic. But the greatest doubt Ana encountered came from Michael Spielman, the founder and director of Abort73.

Ana had understood from someone else with Abort73 that they would be able to hold the Love the Least event in April. But when she e-mailed Mike to confirm, she found out there had been a miscommunication. Mike told her that he admired her desire to plan the event, but he needed to focus on events in bigger cities. "I suspect it will be difficult to fill a venue in Ithaca," he wrote. "I think it's premature to lay out flyers for you, and before we could even come at all, I would need to be convinced that you had legitimate means of filling the auditorium."

Ana was stunned. "I thought, *We put all this effort into this, and now we're not going to be able to do it. What am I going to tell everyone?* I felt all this pressure. So I used the pressure to call up the team and say, 'We're really gonna do this.'" Ana and her team kept planning, knowing there was no guarantee that Mike's team would come.

A few weeks later, Ana e-mailed Mike with an update on their fund-raising and promotion and with details about which churches had committed to being involved. She also suggested that it would be helpful for them to have a definite response from him and Abort73 about whether they could come.

"We know Ithaca is a relatively small town," she wrote, "but we humbly ask you to please keep in mind that Gideon defeated the Midianites with only three hundred men, that Jesus fed five thousand with only five loaves of bread and two fish, and that the Lord Himself was born in a very small town. Thank you very much."

In addition to her detailed e-mail to Mike, Ana's dad stepped in. He sent Mike an e-mail saying, "I'm supporting her. They really want to do this, and it's real." That validation, along with the concrete plans Ana was making, helped Mike make the commitment to come to the event.

Loving the Least

Ana Zimmerman's goal was to have five hundred people come to Love the Least—Ithaca and raise more than four thousand dollars for the event and a donation to Abort73. In the end, almost three hundred and fifty people came to the event and Ana's team raised more than six thousand dollars.

Not everything went as Ana had wanted. Not quite as many people came to the event as she had hoped. Her vision of like-minded people working alongside each other as a team never materialized as she'd wanted. But Love the Least brought greater unity to Christians in Ithaca, crossed many of the denominational and age-group barriers, raised awareness about justice for the unborn, and raised money so that awareness would continue to grow across the country and the world.

Mike Spielman—initially hesitant to get involved in a fifteen-year-old girl's project—sent us an e-mail summarizing the event from his perspective.

Ana was relentless in her determination to bring us out there, despite all the hoops we made her jump through and all my efforts to convince her that this event might not be possible in Ithaca. Thankfully, she didn't give up—despite many discouragements.

Almost immediately after we committed, Ana learned that the venue she had a verbal reservation for was actually booked by someone else. Ana and her team quickly found another location (which providentially put the event at Cornell University) and raised the extra funds needed to hire a sound company to set up and man the system (since we were in a hundred-year-old chapel with almost no AV capabilities).

Despite freezing rain that night, despite the parking garage being a five- to ten-minute walk from the chapel, despite being up against the Final Four, we had a great turnout, and I heard from people over and over that nothing like this had ever happened before in Ithaca, an event that brought so many churches together. It was truly a remarkable weekend—a testimony to God's goodness and the eternal value of doing hard things.

As Ana points out, it's not enough to have high expectations—we need to have high expectations for the right reasons. "It's an incredible privilege to serve God and do what He is doing," she says. "Don't take it lightly!"

One film at a time: John's story

The moment had arrived. Everyone was waiting for the announcement of the grand prize winner of the San Antonio Independent Christian Film Festival (SAICFF)—a tremendous honor among independent Christian filmmakers, with a cash prize of $101,000.

Nineteen-year-old filmmaker John Moore was certain he knew which film would win: *Fireproof,* the Kendrick brothers' film that had already grossed millions in theaters. Sure enough, *Fireproof* was called out—but as a runner-up.

John's mind was spinning, trying to figure out who the winner could be. Then he heard the announcer call out: *"The Widow's Might!"* The auditorium erupted with the roar of applause. John moved mechanically toward the stage. He couldn't believe it. He must have misheard...

HeuMoore Productions

John's journey to the San Antonio Independent Christian Film Festival began in 2004. He and his friend David Heustis formed HeuMoore Productions with the intent of making movies. "Our goal was the spotlight," John says, laughing. "Our quality was your average YouTube video."

HeuMoore Productions faced major obstacles from the start. John's family moved to Texas while David stayed in Alaska. Not only did they have little equipment or money, but also the two halves of the production company lived thousands of miles apart.

"That's when I realized excellence isn't something measured in dollars and cents and that work ethic can't be bound by technology or time," John says. "The foundation of all filmmaking is the most inexpensive and accessible part: the script. So I used all my available money to buy books on filmmaking—specifically, screenwriting."

At this point, John was fourteen years old.

In 2005, John completed his first professionally formatted screenplay. An epic western? A tender tearjerker? No, it was a fifteen-minute comedy piece starring John's siblings. About that time, David's family relocated to Texas. The two friends shot the picture, called *What a Blast,* and shared it with an online film-making group.

That's when the relatively small hard thing of completing a short film met the big hard thing of swallowing pride. The film received honest and blunt criticism from filmmakers John respected. "They were condemning aspects of a project I had spent months writing and planning," he says. "But I was able to accept it because I knew that *What a Blast* was not our end goal. If our goal was growth, we could love criticism."

Keeping On

John and David took the lessons they'd learned from *What a Blast* and applied them to their next film project: *Bubble Trouble.* But when the two friends looked at the final product, they weren't impressed with their progress.

"We were disappointed," John remembers. "It seemed like an awful lot of effort for not a whole lot of improvement."

Even so, John and David entered *Bubble Trouble* in the film festival in San Antonio—and the audiences loved it. It came in second place for Audience Choice Award out of fifty semifinalists. John and David knew they were going in the right direction.

Over the next two years, the two friends were on and off the filmmaking trail, making two more short films in 2006 and 2007. As time went on, they made new connections, and their production crew expanded to include other gifted teens.

But while both films improved on his earlier efforts, John

began to face some of the side effects of doing hard things: acclaim—and complacency.

"I was receiving more recognition and accolades from people than were probably good for me," he told us in a recent e-mail. "I really had to get out from my own community and seek out strong, objective criticism of my projects. That was extremely hard for me to do. I had a solid reputation where I was. I felt like I had arrived. "

When John showed his short films to secular film professionals and asked for honest feedback, they gave him exactly what he was looking for.

John's summary of that process: "It was torture."

Besides outright rejecting the Christian message in John's films, the professionals pointed out flaw after flaw in every part of the production—from scripting to dialogue, acting to cinematography, DVD menus to cover art.

But at the end of these conversations, most of them would ask, "By the way, how old are you?" They were shocked to hear John was seventeen. At the end of this process, John and David realized they could either plateau or grow.

They decided to grow.

The Widow's Might

In 2008, John began working on a new film project. Never one to aim small, John decided he wanted to shoot the film with a bleeding edge piece of camera technology that costs roughly ten times what most teens spend on their first car—the RED camera.

The film was called *The Widow's Might*. Even in retrospect, it sounds crazy. It was a musical; it was a western; it was a political film; it was their first feature-length film—and they had only four months to complete it. But when John showed the finished screenplay to David, David got excited as well.

The movie was about an elderly widow about to lose her home because of tax foreclosure. When two teens learn about it, they try to stop it—enlisting family and friends to make a film educating their town on the issue. In more than a few ways, the film's story line mirrored reality for John and David. The task was daunting.

"We were a team of crazies, cynics, dreamers, artists, visionaries, and realists," John says of the young people who made up HeuMoore Productions. "The two traits we all had in common were our lack of experience and our desire to be mentored."

John and David immediately sought out more experienced men to help with the production—with things like cinematography, lighting, sound, and financing. They weren't looking for people to lift responsibility from their shoulders; they wanted others to help them take the steps themselves.

"The equation was simple," John says. "They would get a team of young people with creativity and passion who were willing to listen to them and respect their experience, and we got a team of very knowledgeable men who would be patient with us and overlook our sometimes embarrassing levels of ignorance."

For several labor-filled months, John and his team secured locations, locked down contracts with various professionals, and prepared for the hardest thing they'd ever done. When it came time to shoot, crew members, facility managers, and local officials were shocked to discover that the writer and director of the film was eighteen, the producer was nineteen, the visual designer was seventeen, and a majority of the grips and cast were teens as well.

At one point John was close to giving up on the whole thing. Now he can't help but remember what Thomas Edison once said: "Many of life's failures are people who did not realize how close they were to success when they gave up." John and his exhausted team submitted the disc to the festival the night of the deadline.

"The project started with me in a room on a computer for hours on end, then David joined in," says John. "At the end, it was the same: both of us, hunched over our keyboards day and night, stressed and completely worn out. There were computer crashes, missing files, regrets about script decisions, and editing around poor acting. Anybody who thinks filmmaking is glamorous is dead wrong."

But the night of the 2009 SAICFF Awards Ceremony, sitting among Christian film giants like Dean Jones, Ken Wales, Alex and Stephen Kendrick, and Kirk Cameron, John had a sense of accomplishment. They had gone far beyond their initial goal of finishing the project. Now they were finalists for the largest cash prize for filmmaking in North America—and the next thing John knew, they had won.

As John walked out on the stage that night to receive the reward he had worked so hard for, his mind was still trying to catch up. "In that moment, the feeling of triumph was greater than anything I'd ever experienced," he says. "The team all stood on that stage, with thousands of people cheering us on. It wasn't my victory; it was *our* victory."

Fade Out

If HeuMoore Productions had a motto, it would be taken from the advice of fellow independent film producer Stephen Kendrick: "Excellence is always excelling."

John explains: "The temptation to feel like we've arrived is always there, but we have an advantage. Four years in a row, we created films that didn't receive the praise we wanted from the professional world. Four years in a row, we created films that we learned and grew from. Four years in a row, we looked at the project, dusted ourselves off, and started over. No lights, no stage, no big cash prize. Just hours on end spent hunched over keyboards in a dimly lit room."

It took another nine months for HeuMoore Productions to prepare the film for DVD and put it in the hands of consumers. Now they are preparing for another feature film. The first step is to go back to *The Widow's Might* and go over every single thing that they know is wrong with it.

When we asked John to address the question of pride in doing hard things, he offered a great perspective: "I always get the greatest feeling after doing something hard. God has designed this intense emotional reaction to inspire us to repeat the things we've done right. It's a feeling we never get when we cheat or cut corners, only through true character. This kind of God-given gladness inspires others to do great things as well.

"If you give *yourself* credit for those moments of tremendous achievement, the satisfaction you get will lose its contagious nature. And when you are defeated, it's purely you who takes the blame. Trusting in God results in thankfulness to God when you've 'won.' And if you fail, you know you haven't been defeated, because God is undefeatable. You can keep going. Only by giving God the praise in our victories can we gladly praise God in our defeats as well."

But if you really want to get John going on something other than film, just ask him if we ever finish hard things. "The answer is a resounding no!" he says. "So many people feel that once you reach a level of accomplishment, everything else just falls into place. The fact is, even if you're talented, it takes perseverance to sustain that talent. The famous playwright Noël Coward once said, 'You've got talent. Thousands of people have talent. I might as well congratulate you for having eyes in your head. The one and only thing that counts is: do you have staying power?'

"It's easy to confuse 'do hard things' with the idea of 'do big things.' A push-up isn't a big thing. Winning a championship is. But doing push-ups when you don't feel like it is what it takes to win in a championship fight.

"*The Widow's Might* is one hard thing I've done, and at the time, it was the championship prize fight of my life. Having dozens of people, hundreds of extras, and hundreds of thousands of dollars at my disposal was huge. But right now I'm writing a screenplay. It's hours and hours of pounding away, erasing my own work, and starting over. This is a quiet time, with no glamour, no glory.

"While some see *The Widow's Might* as a great accomplishment, it's really not. It's the *result* of a great accomplishment: forming a team of young people equally committed to a tremendously difficult vision. The rest—gaining the trust of investors, developing a bleeding edge workflow, and turning around a feature film in four months—well, that was a piece of cake.

"I want my life to be marked not by successes of dollar signs and gold trophies (don't get me wrong—those are always welcome!), but by successes in character. A life marked by doing very, very hard things."

MAKING IT RAIN

It is the end of an amazing conference in the suburbs of Washington DC. We are waiting backstage as our brother Joel and the worship team lead the audience of thirty-five hundred teens, parents, and youth workers in a final chorus of "Reign in Us" by Starfield:

> Come cleanse us like a flood and send us out
> So the world may know you reign, you reign in us.

As the music and voices fade away, we make our way onto the stage to close the day and send everyone back out to their homes, churches, and schools. The expectation in the room is palpable. The attendees want to get started doing hard things for God's glory. They want to make a difference in their communities. They want to change the world.

We hope that our closing activity will give them a vision for what that looks like.

We tell the audience that we are going to make it rain...inside the building. Some of them look bewildered. Others smile and exchange knowing glances—they have done this before.

We divide the room into sections. At our cue, certain sections will rub their hands together. Others will snap their fingers. Others will pat their legs.

First, you hear the soft rustling of wind as hundreds of hands begin to rub together. Then the gentle pattering of rain as one section after another begins snapping their fingers. The intensity builds as a shower of leg patting becomes a downpour of clapping—culminating in a violent thunderstorm as everyone claps their hands and stomps their feet all at once.

The noise is deafening for a few seconds. Then we slowly bring it back down, working through the actions in reverse order. A split second of silence is reached before the audience bursts into enthusiastic applause.

It worked. It sounded like rain.

"You just made it rain in this building!" we announce. "But here's the point: at times you may feel that the hard things you're doing can't make a difference—just like a solitary finger snap seems so quiet and one raindrop seems so insignificant. But when you have an entire generation snapping their fingers, when you have an entire generation being faithful in their own spheres with their own gifts and opportunities..."

Without any cue, the audience starts snapping their fingers, then patting their legs, then clapping, then stomping...

...and those single raindrops become a flood.

100 HARD THINGS

We love the fact that rebelutionaries are doing far too many hard things to include them all in this book. But as an excuse to share some more—and to get you started in figuring out what hard thing to tackle next—here are 100 real-life examples of hard things young people like you have done. For more ideas or to share your own, visit TheRebelution.com.

1. Sent post cards to shut-ins at my church.
2. Memorized a whole book of the Bible.
3. Called my dad on his birthday after my parents got divorced.
4. Made care packages for members of the military.
5. Didn't text for a week and used my extra time to read the Bible.
6. Worked up to one hundred push-ups in four weeks.
7. Saved my first kiss for my wedding day.
8. Made meals for a new mom and cleaned her kitchen while she slept.
9. Sold all the clothes I didn't need and gave the money to charity.
10. Made small gifts and distributed them at a nursing home on Christmas Eve.
11. Let my brother win an argument.

12. Wrote a note of encouragement to the principal of my school.

13. Kept a daily journal of what God was teaching me over a year.

14. Put on a concert at church and raised two thousand dollars for a missionary family in Mexico.

15. Asked my parents to come to church with me.

16. Wrote a song and recorded it in a studio.

17. Hosted a Bible study for kids in my neighborhood.

18. Got certified with the American Heart Association to perform CPR and first aid.

19. Started teaching piano lessons.

20. Learned Spanish.

21. Worked as a camp counselor for kids with disabilities.

22. Donated ten inches of hair to Locks of Love—twice!

23. Sponsored a child through Compassion International (compassion.com).

24. Ran a marathon.

25. Volunteered on a political campaign.

26. Stopped spending money on fast food and coffee and then donated that money to an orphanage.

27. Started a dance and drama team at my church.

28. Fasted from TV for a month.

29. Donated blood to the Red Cross.

30. Wrote a letter to the editor of my local paper.

31. Served as a nursery volunteer in my church.

32. Was the team leader of the Relay for Life for the American Cancer Society (cancer.org).

33. Apologized.

34. Read a book out loud to my younger siblings.

35. Went on a mission trip to an Indian reservation.
36. Moved away from home to be near my ill brother.
37. Started a book club for young women in my church.
38. Rode one thousand miles on my bicycle in six months.
39. Planned and led a rim-to-rim Grand Canyon backpacking trip.
40. Took banana bread to our neighbors.
41. Repaired my relationship with my mom.
42. Invited someone I find annoying to hang out with me and my friends.
43. Volunteered once a week for an elementary-school tutoring program.
44. Designed and made modest but fashionable clothes.
45. Started an overseas adoption ministry at my church.
46. Prayed out loud in a group.
47. Wrote to persecuted Christians through PrisonerAlert.com
48. Wrote letters to representatives in Congress.
49. Prayed with someone in the school hallway.
50. Practiced my musical instrument every day.
51. Started an after-school Bible club in a public elementary school.
52. Sat with a widow at church who had been sitting alone.
53. Ran errands for my parents.
54. Wrote an encouraging letter to my youth pastor.
55. Stopped complaining.
56. Set a bedtime for myself and kept to it.
57. Asked my pastor a question that's been bothering me even though I felt silly.
58. Kept up with the news and prayed about world events.

59. Asked an older Christian friend what area she thought I needed to grow in most.
60. Wrote my parents a letter thanking them for all they do.
61. Took notes at church and reviewed them during the week.
62. Wrote down long-term goals for my life and prayed about them regularly.
63. Gave up my Saturday morning sleep-ins to volunteer at a soup kitchen.
64. Started a regular exercise program.
65. Made over one hundred and fifty apple pies (twice) for a mission trip fund-raiser.
66. Started a pro-life group at my school.
67. Stopped gossiping.
68. Organized a group of friends to pick up trash in my neighborhood.
69. Collected used baby items and donated them to a crisis pregnancy center.
70. Supported a family member who struggles with depression.
71. Learned guitar and accompanied my youth group's praise choir.
72. Asked my friends not to curse around me.
73. Prayed for the kid at school who mistreats me.
74. Bought a carnation from a woman on the street and talked with her.
75. Trained with Child Evangelism Fellowship (cefonline.com).
76. Baby-sat for a single mom who couldn't pay me much.

77. Started an organization that buys ultrasound machines for pregnancy centers.
78. Led "See You at the Pole" at my school (syatp.com).
79. Started an evangelistic Bible study for my volleyball team.
80. Hosted a 30 Hour Famine through World Vision (worldvision.org).
81. Volunteered in an after-school program at a homeless shelter.
82. Tutored four children while their mom recovered from a stroke.
83. Asked my stepsister out for a soda even though we don't get along.
84. Stopped making mean and sarcastic jokes.
85. Set a budget for my finances and stuck to it.
86. Started my own flower business.
87. Played guitar for hospice patients.
88. Took a group of younger kids to a fast-food place and talked about Christ.
89. Organized citywide baby showers for a crisis pregnancy center.
90. Got up earlier than usual in the morning to read my Bible.
91. Set up a prayer station in a city park and offered to pray for people.
92. Asked local businesses if I could volunteer my time to help them.
93. Became an AWANA leader (awana.org).
94. Befriended an exchange student at college.

95. Ended a relationship that wasn't healthy.
96. Refused a part in a play because certain lines in the script violated my conscience.
97. Made an extra plate of food to take to an elderly neighbor.
98. Raised an assistance dog through Guide Dogs of America (guidedogsofamerica.org).
99. Shared a meal with a homeless man and listened to his story.
100. Competed in the National Bible Bee (biblebee.org).

DISCUSSION QUESTIONS

One of the great things God is doing through the Rebelution is uniting young people to do hard things together. We've found that linking arms with like-minded friends is one of the best ways to figure out what hard things God is calling us to do. It's also one of the best ways to become more like Christ in our actions and attitudes. And as you may have already discovered, working with others to do hard things—or simply to get encouragement and ideas for your own project—can be a lot of fun.

So as you start (or continue) doing hard things, we encourage you to get together with a group of friends and talk about what it looks like to do hard things right where God has placed you. You can use the following questions as a personal study guide, but they have been designed especially for group discussion. We've tried to come up with questions that will help you revisit the big ideas of each chapter as well as talk about how they apply to you and your group of fellow rebelutionaries.

Want some advice for making the conversation really worthwhile? Here you go: Pray and invite Jesus to be at the center of your group. Be as honest as you can with each other. Look it up in the Bible when you've got a question. Treat your time together as a launching pad for action in doing hard things.

The group of disciples who surrounded Jesus went on to turn the world upside down. We can't wait to hear what you and your friends are going to do!

Your fellow rebelutionaries,

Alex and Brett Harris

Chapter 1
You Are Here: Opening the Door to Your
Own Rebelution

This book is about taking the next step in your personal *rebelution* against society's low expectations for teens. As young people around the world have discovered, doing hard things is the most satisfying—and exciting—way to live. *Start Here* will help you get started right where you are.

1. How do you respond to the idea of "a teenage rebellion against low expectations" (page 2)?
2. If you have read *Do Hard Things,* how has it changed your perspective on the teen years? Has it changed the way you think or act in any way? If so, how?
3. What is your biggest hope for what you get out of this book? What do you hope for as you begin, or continue, to do hard things?
4. If you were writing a question for this book, what would it be?

Chapter 2
Getting Started: What That First Step Looks Like

Doing hard things to glorify God knocks selfishness out of the picture. We can follow God's calling without worrying about whether we get noticed for it. Being a leader or being a follower, doing small hard things or doing big hard things, accomplishing something big right now or preparing for the future—all this is secondary to having an attitude that is open to God's direction and purpose.

Keeping this in mind will help you answer the question we

all ask at some point: *Where do I start?* This chapter offers ideas about how to move forward for the right reasons.

1. How does our attitude toward doing something change when we do it to glorify God? Why?

2. Do you know what hard thing God is calling you to do? If you do, what is it and why is it important to you? If you don't, what do you think is the next step in figuring it out?

3. What small hard things is God calling you to do before (or while) you do big hard things?

4. When has someone else's willingness to do a small hard thing made a difference in your life?

5. Go back and look over the stories of Elisabeth, Charity, Matthew, Hannah, and Ian. Which of these people do you identify with most? Why?

6. What's the *one* biggest thing that's keeping you from moving ahead and doing something hard? If God were sitting beside you, what do you think He would tell you about this problem? If you are in a group, what can the other group members do to help you take the next step?

Chapter 3
When You Have a Great Idea: Practical Help for Making It Work

Making a plan. Getting people on your side. Raising money. These are some of the practical issues that have to be considered when you're starting a big project. This chapter offers tips that have helped teens get their projects underway.

1. Where would you say you are right now in getting your project going? Clear on your goal but not sure how to go for it? Moving along nicely? Some progress but feeling stuck?

2. Here are some questions to ask yourself as you get started:
   - What are my limits?
   - What do I bring to the table? What can others contribute?
   - What are others already doing? What can I learn from them?
   - Who knows more than I do about this?
   - What can I read about this topic?
   - What is my goal?
   - What do I need to do first to move from planning to doing?

3. Which is the most relevant question for where you are at right now? How would you answer that question?

4. What are the practical realities you're facing as you get started on your project?

5. How do your parents feel about your project? Your friends?

6. What comes to mind when you think of telling people about your project? Do you think it will be easier to approach people you know or to approach strangers? Why?

7. How much money is your project going to cost? What ideas do you have about coming up with that money? (Fund-raising ideas can be fun to brainstorm as a group.)

Chapter 4: Side Effects May Occur:
Handling the Changes That Come
with Doing Hard Things

Doing hard things will bring challenges that you never expected.
The good news is that God invites you to grow closer to Him as
you deal with the effects of doing hard things. The changes you
go through as a person are part of what God has called you to—
and they're part of doing hard things.

1. Briefly describe a time when you received affirmation
    for doing hard things. How did you respond? How did
    the affirmation make you feel?

2. What are some ways that rebelutionaries can use the
    attention they receive to glorify God? How does an
    accomplishment like Zac Sunderland's bring glory to
    God (see pages 49–51)?

3. How have you struggled with pride as you've done hard
    things?

4. In this chapter *busyness* is defined as having a lot to do
    and *fruitfulness* as accomplishing something of eternal
    significance. How have you seen the difference between
    busyness and fruitfulness in your own life?

5. What changes could you make in your day (take today
    or yesterday, for example) that would give you more
    time to be fruitful rather than just busy?

6. If anyone has asked you for an interview about some-
    thing hard you've done, how did that go? What can you
    do to prepare for that possibility in the future? Do you
    think doing interviews is something that will come
    easily for you? Why or why not?

Chapter 5
Matters of First Importance: Keeping God in Focus
Every Step of the Way

There's something more important than doing hard things for God. It's knowing Him. It's enjoying Him. It's loving Him. It's being with Him. This isn't to discourage you from doing hard things—not at all! It's to encourage you to do hard things while keeping your relationship with God your highest priority. As you draw closer to God, you'll have the strength and wisdom to do even more hard things for His glory.

1. Has doing hard things been good or bad for your relationship with God? Explain.

2. If someone looked at your thoughts and activities yesterday, would he or she say that it appeared God was the center of your life? Why or why not?

3. "Putting God at the center of our lives is not a vague act of obedience. It is the only sensible response—to Someone we need and long to know more" (page 67). Would you say your obedience to God comes more from a vague sense of guilt or a desire for relationship? Why?

4. Think about your motives for doing hard things. To what extent are they about glorifying God? To what extent are they about glorifying you? How do you handle these mixed motivations?

5. Grace from Maryland says, "It's a battle of heart attitude, for if my heart isn't in the right place before God, my actions are worthless. It's a battle to...follow His plans for my life, especially when they don't make sense" (page 72). How do you relate to these words?

6. What, if anything, needs to change about the way you are approaching hard things so that you can keep growing in your relationship with God?

Chapter 6
When the Doing Gets Tough: Keeping On in the Middle of Hard Things

One of the myths about teenagers is that teens don't have the toughness to stick with something when it gets difficult. But this is one of the myths we have to bust if we want to do something for God—and change society's perception of teenagers.

Problems *will* come as we do hard things. Instead of being surprised by them, we can know that persistence in the middle of hard things is a key to achieving our goal.

1. Think back to when you first had the idea for your big project. In what ways are you even more excited now about what you're doing? In what ways are you more discouraged?

2. "Overcoming discouragement requires that we continually remind ourselves that growth is worth the pain" (page 77). Do you agree with this statement? Why?

3. Describe a time when you tried to do something hard for God and it didn't work out the way you planned. As you look back now, in what ways can you see God's work in that situation?

4. Picture a line that takes you from the beginning of your project to right now. The higher the line is, the better you feel about your project. The lower it is, the more discouraged you are. Describe and/or draw the course

of this line. What do you think God would say to you
at your highest point? at your lowest point?

5. How are you feeling about the changes *in yourself* as
    a result of doing hard things? Are you surprised?
    disappointed? finding that you haven't really thought
    about it?

6. At the outset, what were your expectations—personally,
    spiritually, and relationally—for doing hard things? In
    what ways have your expectations been helpful to you?
    In what ways might they have hurt you?

Chapter 7
The Guts Factor: How to Move Against the Crowd— and Why

If you dare to attempt hard things for God, some of the people in
your life might think you're great. Others might think you're
crazy. One thing is sure: doing hard things is going to have an
effect on your relationships. Do you have the guts to stick with
what God is calling you to?

1. Since you started doing hard things, has anyone criti-
    cized you for missing out on "normal" teenage life?
    If so, what was said? How did you respond?

2. Would you say that now you are having more fun, less
    fun, or the same amount of fun as you had before doing
    hard things? How has your view of "fun" changed, if at
    all?

3. How has doing hard things changed your friendships
    with, or your reputation among, other young people?

4. Erika (see page 97) describes the harsh reaction she got

from teachers and students for promoting a pro-life position. When has persecution affected you?

5. "Our goal as Christians is not to avoid getting into trouble. It's also not to *try* to get into trouble. Our goal is to get into the *right kind* of trouble" (page 99). How can you tell the difference between the "right kind of trouble" and the wrong kind?

6. Describe a book, movie, song, or website that you're not sure is a good influence on you. Get advice from others in the group about whether they think it will bring you closer to God or push you away from Him—and about practical steps you can take about it.

Chapter 8
Now What? When Doing Is Done

Whew! When you're done with a big hard thing, you might feel proud, let down, tired, or incredibly energized. What are you going to do with those feelings? What are you going to do next? Finishing one hard thing and moving on to another reminds us that being a rebelutionary is not just about what happens while you're a teen. It's also about preparing for an entire lifetime of loving and glorifying God.

1. When have you seen "godly excitement over doing a hard thing" lead not to pride but to humility—either in your life or in someone else's life?

2. When you've come to the end of a big project, have you ever had a problem with selfish pride? If so, describe it.

3. Describe a time you fell back into a bad habit after doing something hard. Did you get out of it again? If so, how?

4. Andrew filled a bag with stuff from his room he wanted
   to get rid of. Kristin stopped sitting with her old crowd
   at lunch. Justin confessed to his boss about stealing
   books. Think about one way you want to move beyond
   your old ways of thinking and acting. What practical
   action could you take to make a permanent change in
   your life?

5. Think about the time when you finish the project you
   are currently working on. How are you going to celebrate? How are you going to rest up? Do you have an
   idea of what hard thing you're going to do next?

6. Has doing hard things ever made you excited about
   tackling an even bigger challenge? Talk about it.

Chapter 9
Putting It All Together: Two Stories
That Will Answer All Your Questions
(or at Least Give You Some Great Ideas)

Ana Zimmerman raised more than six thousand dollars to help
end the injustice of abortion. John Moore wrote, produced, and
directed his own film, going on to win the grand prize at the San
Antonio Independent Christian Film Festival. In this chapter,
Ana and John provide a step-by-step look at their projects and
how God used those hard things for His glory.

1. What part of Ana's story do you identify with the
   most? Why?

2. What part of John's story do you identify with the
   most? Why?

3. Ana points out that it's not enough to have high
   expectations—we need to have high expectations

for the right reasons (page 128). What does this mean?

4. John tells us he was able to accept criticism because he knew that his first film was not his main goal: "If our goal was growth, we could love criticism" (page 130). How have you found that statement to be true in your own life?

5. John reminds us that "it's easy to confuse 'do hard things' with the idea of 'do big things.' A push-up isn't a big thing. Winning a championship is. But doing push-ups when you don't feel like it is what it takes to win in a championship fight" (page 135). Would you say you're doing push-ups right now, or are you in the middle of a championship fight? Why? When have you confused doing hard things with doing big things?

6. What are some practical ideas you got out of Ana's and John's stories?

Chapter 10
Making It Rain

Start Here wraps up with the image of thousands of young people making it rain—indoors! After all, when individuals offer their gifts to God, anything can happen.

1. What story in the book was most challenging to you? Why?

2. Has the message of doing hard things inspired you to believe that one young person can make a difference in a generation? Why or why not?

3. *Start Here* gives ideas and stories featuring the beginning, middle, and end of hard projects. What are some

of the practical things you learned about each of those stages?

4. What is one question you would add to this book? How would you (or your group) answer it?

5. A friend asks you at lunch: "So how do you start doing hard things?" What do you say?

NOTES

Chapter 2

1. To read more about Hope 2 Others, see Alex and Brett Harris, *Do Hard Things: A Teenage Rebellion Against Low Expectations* (Colorado Springs, CO: Multnomah, 2008), 199–203.
2. For other ideas on collaboration, see chapter 7 of *Do Hard Things*.
3. From a personal conversation with the authors. Used by permission.

Chapter 3

1. All quotes about Joshua Guthrie and Dollar for a Drink are taken from Mark Kelly, "Teen's Vision Brings Water to Darfur," *Baptist Press,* March 23, 2009, www.bpnews.net/bpnews.asp?ID=30122 (accessed October 22, 2009). For more information about Dollar for a Drink, see www.dollarforadrink.org.
2. See also Harris, *Do Hard Things,* 121–3.
3. John Maxwell, *The 21 Irrefutable Laws of Leadership,* 10th ann. ed. (Nashville: Thomas Nelson, 2007), 115.
4. For more ideas on using technology, see Harris, *Do Hard Things,* 123–4.

Chapter 4

1. Scott Thompson, "Teen Becomes Youngest to Sail Solo Around the World," *CNN.com,* July 17, 2009,http://www.cnn.com/2009/US/07/16/teen.sails.around.world (accessed November 25, 2009).

2. From personal correspondence with the authors. Used by permission.

3. From personal correspondence with the authors. Used by permission.

4. Walter Chantry, *David: Man of Prayer, Man of War* (Carlisle, PA: Banner of Truth, 2007), 184–5.

5. Corrie ten Boom, quoted in Pamela Rosewell Moore, *The Five Silent Years of Corrie ten Boom* (Grand Rapids: Zondervan, 1986), 92.

6. C. J. Mahaney, "Are You Busy?" Sovereign Grace Ministries, November 12, 2008, www.sovereigngraceministries.org/Blog/post/how-busyness-and-laziness-coexist-cj-mahaney.aspx (accessed October 22, 2009).

7. From a personal conversation with the authors. Used by permission.

8. Dallas Willard, "Key to the Keys of the Kingdom," Dallas Willard, www.dwillard.org/articles/artview.asp?artID=40 (accessed October 22, 2009). Originally published in Dallas Willard, *The Great Omission* (San Francisco: HarperCollins, 2006).

Chapter 5

1. J. D. Douglas and others, eds., *New Bible Dictionary* (Downers Grove, IL: InterVarsity, 1962), 553.

Chapter 7

1. From a personal e-mail to the authors. Used by permission.

2. Broken Cords, "Frequently Asked Questions," www.brokencords.com/about/faq (accessed October 22, 2009).

3. Stacy Parent, "Teens Work to End Human Trafficking," *The Baytown [Texas] Sun,* July 14, 2009, http://baytownsun.com/story/46309/ (accessed October 22, 2009).

4. Parent, "Teens Work to End Human Trafficking."

5. From a personal e-mail to the authors. Used by permission.

6. For other thoughts on going against the crowd, see chapter 9 of Harris, *Do Hard Things*.

7. In Luke 6:22–23, Jesus speaks to a great multitude of people, saying, "Blessed are you when people hate you and when they exclude you and revile you and spurn your name as evil, on account of the Son of Man! *Rejoice in that day, and leap for joy,* for behold, your reward is great in heaven; for so their fathers did to the prophets." In Acts 5:40–42, the apostle Paul describes the experiences of Peter and the other apostles, writing: "When [the council] had called in the apostles, they beat them and charged them not to speak in the name of Jesus, and let them go. Then they left the presence of the council, *rejoicing that they were counted worthy to suffer dishonor for the name.* And every day, in the temple and from house to house, they did not cease teaching and preaching Jesus as the Christ." And as Paul told Timothy, "Everyone who wants to live a godly life in Christ Jesus will be persecuted" (2 Timothy 3:12, NIV).

Chapter 8

1. For more on the topic of pride, we recommend one of our favorite books, packed with truth and practical insight. It's called *Humility: True Greatness* by C. J. Mahaney (Colorado Springs: Multnomah, 2005).

2. MSNBC.com Video, "Hoops for Hope [*sic*] Builds School in Africa," http://video.msn.com/video.aspx?mkt=enUS&brand= msnbc&vid=3139f97a-e0ed-4133-abcf-f8892e9bd2a4 (accessed October 22, 2009).

3. MSNBC.com Video, "Hoops for Hope [*sic*] Builds School in Africa."

4. Hoops of Hope, "Project Goals & History," www.hoopsofhope.org/project-goals-history.html (accessed October 22, 2009).

Chapter 9

1. All quotes and facts from Ana Zimmerman's and John Moore's stories are from personal conversation and correspondence with the authors unless otherwise noted. Used by permission.

ACKNOWLEDGMENTS

To GT's Kombucha and Snyder of Hanover's hard pretzels—you've seen us through many college papers and, now, this book.

To all the rebelutionaries who submitted their questions, stories, and ideas. You are the reason—and the inspiration—for this book. Thank you.

To all our friends at WaterBrook Multnomah. Thanks for getting (and staying) excited about recruiting and equipping a generation to do hard things.

To our assistant writer and editor, Elisa Stanford. You made writing this book (as full-time college students) possible! Thanks for helping us identify and organize all the questions and examples in the early going, taking the time-intensive book details off our hands, and making the book come alive with stories. It was a joy to work with you.

To our parents and siblings. Thanks for putting up with another crazy book-writing season, even when it meant less time together this past summer. We couldn't do anything we're doing without your love, sacrifice, and hard work. We love you.

To our Lord and Savior, Jesus Christ. *Soli Deo Gloria!*

From Alex: To the love of my life—my wife, Courtney. You not only cheered me on, but you helped me brainstorm answers to questions and craft my responses. Your insights and ideas made their way into so many of these pages. Working together was a dream come true. I can't wait to write a book together someday. I love you.